HIS FINAL
HOURS

HIS FINAL HOURS

W. JEFFREY MARSH

DESERET
BOOK

SALT LAKE CITY, UTAH

Library of Congress Cataloging-in-Publication Data

Marsh, W. Jeffrey.
    His final hours / W. Jeffrey Marsh.
       p. cm.
    Includes bibliographical references.
    ISBN-10 1-57345-645-4
    ISBN-13 978-1-57345-645-6
    1. Jesus Christ—Crucifixion. 2. Jesus Christ—Resurrection. 3. Jesus Christ—Mormon interpretations. 4. Atonement. 5. Spiritual life—Mormon Church. I. Title.

BT453 .M33 2000
232.96—dc21   00-020908

Printed in the United States of America
Malloy Lithographing Incorporated, Ann Arbor, MI
10   9   8   7   6

For Kathie, Jason, Jami, Korey, Kelley, Shaun,
Whitney, Carrie, Stephen, Cami, and Katie

CONTENTS

PREFACE

This book is meant to bear witness of Christ, our Savior, the Son of God, and to do as King Benjamin suggested—express "all the thanks and praise which your whole soul has power to possess" (Mosiah 2:20).

But if there are errors in the way the ideas are expressed, I accept full responsibility. My desire is to share the marvelous insights about life that can be drawn from the final hours of the Savior's life and atoning sacrifice. In dying, he taught us how to live life more abundantly. What he did for us is of transcendent value. Nothing is more important than the Father's plan for our eternal salvation and the Savior's eternal sacrifice that makes it all possible.

The scriptures promise that the time will come when "the knowledge of the Savior shall spread through every nation, kindred, tongue, and people" (Mosiah 3:20). Even with all the millennia that have come and gone, that has not yet happened. My sincere desire is that the new millennium we are entering will be the dawning of just such a blessed day.

ACKNOWLEDGMENTS

No one brings a project like this to fruition without help. Deepest appreciation and thanks go to Cory Maxwell and Suzanne Brady of Deseret Book for their encouragement and editorial help. Special thanks goes to the Deseret Book editorial board for their helpful suggestions and to Rebecca Roesler and Kristen Maetani for their research assistance in checking and cross-checking references. Most important, I wish to thank Elder Neal A. Maxwell, whose prolific and powerful prose about the Savior's atonement has enlightened many.

JERUSALEM

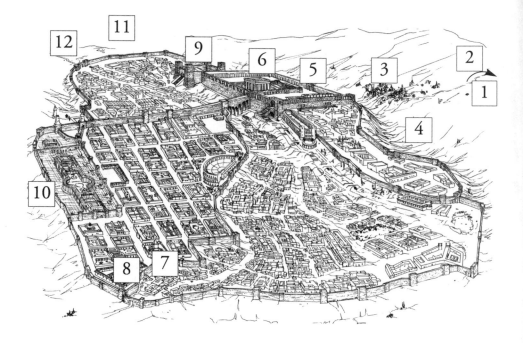

1. Bethany; 2. Mount of Olives; 3. Garden of Gethsemane; 4. Kidron Valley; 5. Golden Gate; 6. The temple; 7. Upper Room, site of the Last Supper; 8. Caiaphas' Palace, site of the Jewish trial; 9. Antonia Fortress, site of the Roman trial; 10. Herod's Palace; 11. Golgotha/Calvary, site of the Crucifixion; 12. Garden Tomb, site of the Resurrection

"BESIDE ME THERE IS NO SAVIOUR"

To this end was I born, and for this cause came I into the world, that I should bear witness unto the truth.
—John 18:37

All truth—and all hope for mankind—is centered in Christ, our Savior, the Son of God. The message of the restored gospel, the glad tidings that angels have shared with mortals, is "that he came into the world, even Jesus, to be crucified for the world, and to bear the sins of the world, and to sanctify the world, and to cleanse it from all unrighteousness; that through him all might be saved" (D&C 76:41–42). "My Father sent me," Jesus declared, "that I might draw all men unto me" (3 Nephi 27:14).

Christ's atoning sacrifice and the events of his final week on earth occurred a long time ago, but the lessons he taught us in his final hours are timeless. He is our only hope for eternal life and happiness: "Beside me there is no saviour" (Isaiah 43:11).

He is our personal redeemer and our only representative to the Father: "Surely he has borne [my] griefs, and carried [my] sorrows; . . . he was wounded for [my] transgressions, he was bruised for [my] iniquities; the chastisement of [my] peace was upon him; and with his stripes [I can be] healed" (Mosiah 14:4–5). We owe him everything.

Because Christ came into our fallen world, we have power to transcend it and enter his celestial realm: "Therefore, whoso repenteth and cometh unto me as a little child, him will I receive, for of such is the kingdom of God. Behold, for such I have laid down my life, and have taken it up again; therefore repent, and come unto me ye ends of the earth, and be saved" (3 Nephi 9:22).

In dying, the Savior taught us how to live. Each event during his atonement, crucifixion, and resurrection teaches us about the Savior's perfect character. His invitation to us to become even as he is was beautifully portrayed during the last few hours of his mortal life. Faced with the most extreme exigencies, he showed us what to do and how to live on a higher spiritual level. As we follow the Savior during his final hours on earth and watch how he dealt with all the injustices thrust upon him, we learn how to prepare ourselves to return to God.

The events surrounding the Savior's final hours on earth can give us a more vibrant testimony and a richer understanding of the living reality of the Son of God. We can come to know that his grace and mercy can bear us up today and that he is aware of each of us personally, loves us individually, and wants us to return home again to the Father's presence. That is his greatest priority (Moses 1:39).

"WHAT THINK YE OF CHRIST?"

Why is Christ "the great, and the last, and the only sure foundation" upon which we should build our lives? (Jacob 4:16). The answers can be multiplied, but the principal answer is that he is the Only Begotten Son of God, our Redeemer. He is the consummate example who showed us the way to perfection. He loves us perfectly. His teachings are eternal principles designed to help us find happiness in this life and eternal joy in the world to come. His atonement overcame death and hell, thus assuring us of immortality and the possibility of eternal life. He has power to bless us. We can have total faith in him. He is an exalted being who has revealed himself to us—only an exalted being can teach us how to become exalted.

It matters more than anything else what we think of Christ. When confronted by the Pharisees, the Savior asked, "What think ye of Christ? whose son is he?" (Matthew 22:42). He put a similar question to his disciples: "Whom do men say that I the Son of man am? . . . whom say ye that I am?" (Matthew 16:13, 15). The children of Israel were asked, "Who is on the Lord's side?" (Exodus 32:26). The Nephites were asked, "Have ye received his image in your countenances?" (Alma 5:14). In general conference President David O. McKay asked Latter-day Saints, "What think ye of Christ?" and then declared: "To the Church, and to the world, I repeat this question as being the most vital, the most far-reaching query in this unsettled, distracted world. . . . What you sincerely in your heart think of Christ will determine what you are, will largely determine what your acts will be. No person can study this divine personality, can accept his teachings without becoming conscious of an uplifting and refining influence within himself. . . .

"Christ came to redeem the world from sin. He came with love in his heart for every individual, with redemption and possibility for regeneration for all. By choosing him as our ideal, we create within ourselves a desire to be like him, to have fellowship with him. We perceive life as it should be and as it may be. . . .

"Members of the Church of Christ are under obligation to make the sinless Son of Man their ideal—the one perfect being who ever walked the earth."[1]

To make Christ our ideal, as President McKay suggested, is to follow his example and partake of his Spirit. Modern revelation teaches that those who receive "the testimony of Jesus" with all their hearts will receive the celestial kingdom in the day of judgment (D&C 76:51). To receive the testimony of Jesus means, simply, to receive the Holy Ghost. Because the Father, the Son, and the Holy Ghost are of one mind and one heart, to receive one is to receive the others. To have the mind of Christ means that we become one with him as he is one with his Father. To have his image engraven on our countenances is to have his Spirit with us (Alma 5:19). All of this happens as we allow the Holy Ghost into our lives. The Holy Spirit will lead us to a greater understanding of Christ and teach us about God (D&C 84:46–47).

MORE THAN A GREAT TEACHER

Someone has said that if Shakespeare came into the room, we would all stand up. But if Jesus Christ came into the room, we would all kneel down and worship him.[2] He is greater than any man who has ever lived on this earth.

Christ came to rescue us from death. He is the only one who did not have to die, because he was the Only Begotten of the Father. There never was and never will be another like Jesus. He was not subject to death, but he did die. He did it for us. He is who he claims to be, namely, the Eternal Son of the Father and the Redeemer of all mankind. Nobody else could save us. That is why we join his Church, keep his commandments, and are baptized in his name. Only he could do what needed to be done. We cannot be neutral where Christ is concerned. We must accept his love and then trust him and follow him. Eternal life cannot be found any other way or in any other person. So "why not speak of the atonement of Christ, and attain to a perfect knowledge of him"? (Jacob 4:12). The story of his life is not just a great story. It is true.

C. S. Lewis eloquently described the Savior's life: "Among these Jews there suddenly turns up a man who goes about talking as if He was God. He claims to forgive sins. He says He has always existed. He says He is coming to judge the world at the end of time. Now let us get this clear. Among Pantheists [those who believe that the universe and the combined forces of nature make up God], . . . anyone might say that he was a part of God, or one with God: there would be nothing very odd about it. But this man, since He was a Jew, could not mean that kind of God. God, in their language, meant the Being outside the world Who had made it and was infinitely different from anything else. . . .

"One part of the claim tends to slip past us . . . I mean the claim to forgive sins: any sins. Now unless the speaker is God, this is really so preposterous as to be comic. We can all understand how a man forgives offences against himself. . . . But what should we make of a man, himself unrobbed and untrodden on, who announced that he forgave you for treading on other men's toes and stealing other men's money? . . . Yet this is what Jesus did. He told people their sins were forgiven, and never waited to consult all the other people whom their sins had undoubtedly injured. . . . This makes sense only if He really was the God whose laws are broken and whose love is wounded in every sin. In the mouth of any speaker who is not God, these words would imply . . . silliness and conceit unrivalled . . . in history. . . .

"I am trying to prevent anyone saying the really foolish thing that people often say about Him: 'I'm ready to accept Jesus as a great moral teacher, but I don't accept His claim to be God.' That is the one thing we must not say. A man who was merely a man and said the sort of things Jesus said would not be a great moral teacher. He would either be a lunatic—on a level with the man who says he is a poached egg—or . . . something worse. You can shut Him up for a fool, you can spit at Him and kill Him as a demon; or you can fall at His feet and call Him Lord and God. But let us not come with any patronising nonsense about His being a great human teacher. He has not left that open to us."[3]

During his lifetime, some despised and rejected him. The more narrow one's view of the Savior is, the more likely such a person is to "consider him a man" (Mosiah 3:9) or to "judge him to be a thing of naught" (1 Nephi 19:9). "Some still settle for regarding Jesus as a mere figure in folklore. Others see Him as a significant moral, but nevertheless mortal, teacher—a Socrates of Samaria, a Plato of Palestine."[4] Yet, he is the most important person in our lives.

When Christ was born, many refused him room (JST Luke 2:7). Today, Jesus stands at the door of our individual lives and knocks (Revelation 3:20). The question he seems to be asking is, "Is there room enough in your heart for me?" Like the wise men who searched diligently to find him, wise-hearted and spiritually minded individuals open that door and prepare the way by making his paths straight (Alma 7:19). That means such individuals remove any obstacles that would prevent God from coming into their lives.

We all need Christ as our guide. President Howard W. Hunter

said, "We should at every opportunity ask ourselves, 'What would Jesus do?' and then be more courageous to act upon the answer. . . . We must know Christ better than we know him; we must remember him more often than we remember him; we must serve him more valiantly than we serve him."[5]

As we learn more of Christ, our adoration will grow, our discipleship will deepen, and our joys will increase. It is more than comforting to know that we, too, can answer as Peter did when he was asked, "Whom say ye that I am?": "Thou art the Christ, the Son of the living God." And perhaps the Savior's response will be the same to us as it was to Peter: "Blessed art thou" (Matthew 16:15–17).

KNOWING HIM

Not all knowledge is of equal value. The highest knowledge we can seek is of our Savior and our Heavenly Father. Our eternal destiny hinges on our willingness to seek after that knowledge: "This is life eternal, that they might know thee the only true God, and Jesus Christ, whom thou hast sent" (John 17:3). Wise men and women still seek him. "I would commend you," urged Moroni, "to seek this Jesus of whom the prophets and apostles have written" (Ether 12:41). And God has provided the means—the holy scriptures and the testimonies of those who have seen him—that all who seek may know that Jesus is the Christ. Everything that has been done in our dispensation, every endeavor associated with the Restoration, has been done for the sole purpose of conveying to the world the great message that Jesus is the Christ.

The Lord has all power. He can work miracles in our lives today. But many have consigned him to history, unwilling to accept the living reality of his guiding hand in today's world (2 Nephi 28:5–6). His ministry is not limited by time. He is "merciful and kind forever" (Moses 7:30).

It may not be essential to know every detail of Jesus' mortal life, but it is critical to understand who he is and what he did for us. Even the four Gospels in the New Testament give us little information about his personal life and few details of his early childhood and youth. We tend to think of the four Gospels as sketches of Christ's life, but the Joseph Smith Translation changes the titles of these four records from "The *Gospel* of St. Matthew," or Mark, or Luke, or John, to "The *Testimony* of St. Matthew," and so on. The Joseph Smith Translation of the Bible, particularly, emphasizes the doctrines of Christ's ministry rather than the details of his life. In fact, Dr. Andrew C. Skinner has noted that the Joseph Smith Translation "gives brilliant and unparalleled illumination to the last few days of the life of Jesus that makes it, by far, the best biblical translation in existence."[6]

The Gospels are not biographies—they are testimonies. And because the four Gospels deal with only thirty-one days of the Savior's thirty-three years of mortal life,[7] they do not even record his greatest teachings or tell us about the most significant miracles he performed:

"Then began he to upbraid the cities wherein most of his mighty works were done, because they repented not: Woe unto thee, Chorazin! woe unto thee, Bethsaida! for if the mighty works, which were done in you, had been done in Tyre and Sidon [non-Israelite cities], they would have repented long ago in sackcloth and ashes" (Matthew 11:20–21). "And there are also many other things which Jesus did, the which, if they should be written every one, I suppose that even the world itself could not contain the books that should be written" (John 21:25).

None of the scriptures tell us what happened in Chorazin or Bethsaida. But the sacred records, the words of the holy prophets, do testify of who Christ is and what he did to secure eternal life for us. They bear a tremendous witness of why he came to earth. When we read the scriptures, we are not just studying them; we are studying about him. All of the scriptures brought forth in the Restoration have been given for one significant reason: to "make known to all kindreds, tongues, and people, that the Lamb of God is the Son of the Eternal Father, and the Savior of the world; and that all men must come unto him, or they cannot be saved" (1 Nephi 13:40).

We know who Christ is. We know whose Son he is. And we know why he came to earth. It's all part of a great plan for our happiness.

NOTES

1. McKay, Conference Report, April 1951, 93, 98.
2. Cited by McKay, Conference Report, October 1950, 168.
3. Lewis, *Mere Christianity*, 54–56.
4. Maxwell, *Even As I Am*, 8.
5. Hunter, "He Invites Us to Follow Him," 5.
6. Skinner, "Restored Light," 16. Elder Bruce R. McConkie of the Quorum of the Twelve Apostles said, "The Joseph Smith Translation, or Inspired Version, is a thousand times over the best Bible now existing on earth" ("The Bible, a Sealed Book," 5).
7. Matthews, *A Bible!* 271.

THE CENTERPIECE
OF THE PLAN OF SALVATION 2

I am the way, the truth, and the life.
—John 14:6

Of all the events in world history, which is the greatest? Of all the weeks that have come and gone, which is the most important to mankind?

Would it not be that event, or that week, which has had an effect on every person who has ever lived? From an eternal perspective, is there any event more important in world history, touching the lives of all mankind, than the atonement and resurrection of Jesus Christ? Without it everything else is both meaningless and useless.

Christ's atonement and resurrection are the centerpiece in God's merciful plan for our happiness and salvation. Christ's sacrifice is the central act in all human history. It affects all people of all ages. As Elder Neal A. Maxwell surmised, "Never has anyone offered so much to so many in so few words as when Jesus said, 'Here am I, send me.'"[1]

Each individual who tastes the sweet gift of forgiveness and experiences the inner peace made possible by the Atonement understands why the week of the atoning sacrifice is more important than all others. Even if a person has never heard of the Savior and does not know anything about him, it is nevertheless true that Christ's final hours affect everyone. That is why every other event and every other moment pale in comparison to Christ's marvelous sacrifice. It is the most transcendent of all events, "the most important single thing that has ever occurred in the entire history of created things; it is the rock foundation upon which the gospel and all other things rest."[2]

The Atonement does things for us we cannot do for ourselves. It is the power emanating from God and our Savior's atonement that hold all things together (D&C 88:41). His mercy, an incredible gift of love, bears us up (2 Nephi 2:8). The grace he extends to us is "an enabling power that allows men and women to lay hold on eternal life and exaltation after they have expended their own best efforts."[3]

The Atonement, which occurred during his final hours, overcame every problem associated with the fall of mankind, collectively and individually. The physical and spiritual deaths brought about by the Fall have been defeated: "For as in Adam all die, even so in Christ shall all be made alive" (1 Corinthians 15:22). His atoning sacrifice cleanses us from sin and will carry us back into the presence of the Father. The question is, Will we be allowed to stay? The answer depends on our willingness to follow Christ's commandments (2 Nephi 31:20). We are truly saved by the "merits, and mercy, and grace of the Holy Messiah" (2 Nephi 2:8), but it is not cheap grace, for there is no exaltation without effort on our part (2 Nephi 25:23).

We must not fail to make the effort to learn of what he did in those final hours. We must not be ignorant of the price he paid for all mankind with his atonement, nor can we choose to disregard it. We can come to know the joy of repentance, made possible through his atonement, and know the peace of heart that comes to those who believe in his resurrection. There is a plan for our happiness and a merciful God who will abundantly pardon all those who seek him (Isaiah 55:6–7).

THE GREAT PLAN OF HAPPINESS

It is more than coincidence that the word *plan* never shows up in the entire Bible one single time. It is possible to read the Bible cover to cover and never know there is a specific plan for our salvation. Satan is thrilled to keep God's plan a secret from us. But after we understand the plan from the perspective of latter-day revelation, portions of it can be seen clearly throughout the Old and the New Testaments. Nevertheless, it cannot be learned from the Bible alone. "The problem with the Bible is not one of language and translation—it is the absence of an adequate and complete manuscript. Hence we need latter-day revelation to teach us what we need to know."[4] God and his plan for our happiness are either revealed from heaven or remain forever unknown (Jacob 4:8).

In the latter-day scriptures of the Restoration, the word *plan* appears thirty-two times. The phrases used by the prophets to describe the plan also bear witness of our Father's great love and concern for us:

"The merciful plan of the great Creator" (2 Nephi 9:6).

"O how great the plan of our God" (2 Nephi 9:13).

"The great and eternal plan of deliverance" (2 Nephi 11:5).

"The great plan of redemption" (Jacob 6:8; Alma 34:31).

"The plan of salvation" (Jarom 1:2; Alma 24:14; Moses 6:62).

"The plan of redemption, which was laid from the foundation of the world" (Alma 12:25).

"The plan of redemption" (Alma 12:26, 30, 32–33; 17:16; 18:39; 29:2; 39:18; 42:11, 13).

"The plan of redemption, which was prepared from the foundation of the world" (Alma 22:13).

"The great plan of the Eternal God" (Alma 34:9).

"The great and eternal plan of redemption" (Alma 34:16).

"The plan of restoration" (Alma 41:2).

"The great plan of salvation" (Alma 42:5).

"The great plan of happiness" (Alma 42:8).

"The plan of mercy" (Alma 42:15).

"The plan of happiness" (Alma 42:16).

"The great plan of mercy" (Alma 42:31).

"And the Gods saw . . . that their plan was good" (Abraham 4:21).

"God's eternal plan" (Official Declaration 2).

The Prophet Joseph Smith said that the plan of salvation is something that ought to occupy our thoughts "day and night" and that because it is of such importance we should expect God to reveal something in reference to it. "What is the object of our coming into existence, then dying and falling away, to be here no more? . . . If we have any claim on our Heavenly Father for anything, it is for knowledge on this important subject."[5]

Our Father does have a plan for our salvation and happiness. It is the only plan of redemption available. There is no other plan, no other way back. And Christ's atonement is at the heart of it all. "I am the way, the truth, and the life," Jesus taught, "no man cometh unto the Father, but by me" (John 14:6). "There is no other way or means whereby man can be saved, only in and through Christ," Alma said, because "he is the life and the light of the world" (Alma 38:9).

In the premortal life we were all present in the Grand Council. We heard the plan explained and saw the Savior chosen. "We sanctioned it."[6] We knew him and loved him long before we were born. We "sang together" and "shouted for joy" when the earth was created and the plan of salvation was made known to us (Job 38:7).

There is now, and always has been, only one plan for our salvation. Satan rebelled against the Father's plan. Satan had no plan to save us. He hates us. It was and always has been his single purpose to oppose the Father's great plan of happiness. He tried to usurp the Father's plan and lead a rebellion to overthrow God (2 Nephi 24:14; Moses 4:1–2). All Satan can offer is misery. But Christ offers us peace, mercy, light, life eternal, and unending joy. God wants us to have the fulness of joy he possesses. And, mercifully, he has given us the ability to choose that joy, for he has given us the freedom to act for ourselves (2 Nephi 10:23).

In Christ's final hours, he paid the price for the salvation of all of us. The Father's plan was so grand that no one was to be excluded: "For behold, he suffereth the pains of all men, yea, the pains of every living creature, both men, women, and children, who belong to the family of Adam" (2 Nephi 9:21). We either take advantage of the gift of mercy Christ offers us through the Father's plan or face the demands of justice and suffer as Christ did. There is no third alternative (D&C 45:1–3; 19:16–19). "Wherefore, how great the importance to make these things known unto the inhabitants of the earth" (2 Nephi 2:8).

UNIQUELY QUALIFIED

Why was Jesus uniquely qualified to be the Savior? Why is he the only way? Four important reasons are described in the scriptures.

First, he alone was worthy because he was sinless (Hebrews 4:15; 9:14; 2 Corinthians 5:21; 1 Peter 1:19; Mosiah 15:5; D&C 20:22). The law of justice forbids any unclean thing to enter the kingdom of God, and because all of us have sinned, all of us would thereby be excluded (2 Nephi 2:5; 1 Nephi 15:34). Because Jesus committed no sin, he was the only one of Heavenly Father's children not bound down by the demands of justice. And because he paid for our sins, he can meet the demands of justice on our behalf (2 Nephi 2:7).

Second, he was foreordained, chosen from the beginning (1 Peter 1:20; Revelation 13:8; Ether 3:14; Moses 4:2; Abraham 3:27).

Third, as the Only Begotten Son of God, he inherited God's power over death (John 10:17–18; 2 Nephi 2:8; Mormon 7:5). He could lay down his life and take it up again. No one else has had power to do that.

Fourth, his atonement is universal. It affects all mankind (2 Nephi 9:7) and all of the Father's creations (D&C 76:40–43).

AN INVITATION TO JOIN IN THE WORK

Although the Atonement is an accomplished fact in that Christ has paid the price for our sins and imperfections, the work of redeeming souls is a continuing effort. He lived, and he lives now. "I am he that liveth, and was dead; and, behold, I am alive for evermore, Amen" (Revelation 1:18).

The work he voluntarily began in the premortal life was not finished in his final hours of mortality. When will it be finished? "Not until he has redeemed and saved every son and daughter of our father

Adam that have been or ever will be born upon this earth to the end of time, except the sons of perdition. That is his mission."[7]

Not only is Christ involved full time in redeeming us—his whole work and his glory is devoted to bringing to pass our exaltation (Moses 1:39)—but he has also invited us to join him in the endeavor. In fact, we promised him, long before we were born, that we would do all in our power to help, as Elder John A. Widtsoe explained:

"In our preexistent state, in the day of the great council, we made a certain agreement with the Almighty. The Lord proposed a plan, conceived by him. We accepted it. Since the plan is intended for all men, we became parties to the salvation of every person under the plan. We agreed, right then and there, to be not only saviors for ourselves but measurably, saviors for the whole human family. We went into a partnership with the Lord. The working out of the plan became then not merely the Father's work, and the Savior's work, but also our work. The least of us, the humblest, is in partnership with the Almighty in achieving the purposes of the eternal plan of salvation.

"That places us in a very responsible attitude towards the human race. By that doctrine, with the Lord at the head, we become saviors on Mount Zion, all committed to the great plan of offering salvation to the untold numbers of spirits. To do this is the Lord's self-imposed duty, this great labor his highest glory. Likewise, it is man's duty, self-imposed, his pleasure and joy, his labor, and ultimately his glory."[8]

The Savior invites us to become saviors with him: "For they were set to be a light unto the world, and to be the saviors of men" (D&C 103:9). The Old Testament prophet Obadiah also foresaw the latter-day work and said that "saviours shall come up on mount Zion [the temple mount] . . . and the kingdom shall be the Lord's" (Obadiah 1:21). The word *saviours* in that verse is plural and not capitalized. It refers to the volunteer corps of latter-day Israelites who would help God accomplish his work (Jacob 5:70–71). And that is our privilege. Imagine! We can, at God's invitation, under his direction, and with his authority, help him accomplish his work. What an incredible opportunity!

We assist him in his work as we become "saviours" in the

unmatched work of redemptive love: sharing the gospel with those who are living and providing eternal ordinances in temples for those who are deceased. President Gordon B. Hinckley exclaimed, "Can there be a greater labor of love than this? It comes more nearly of partaking of the spirit of the Lord himself, who gave his life as a vicarious sacrifice for all of us, than any other work of which I know. It is done in the name of him whose salvation is universal."[9]

We have a great responsibility. We are responsible for all who have lived, all who now live, and all who will yet live. The eternal salvation of the world rests on our shoulders. We will not finish this work "until we have saved ourselves, and then not until we shall have saved all depending upon us."[10]

OUR FATE WITHOUT CHRIST

Have you ever wondered what our fate would have been had the Savior not completed the Atonement? The Fall is so powerful that it has dominion over all. By itself, it would have destroyed the plan. "Wherefore, the first judgment which came upon man [the physical and spiritual death that came as a result of the Fall] must needs have remained to an endless duration" (2 Nephi 9:7). Without the resurrection, we would have remained as unembodied spirits forever. And without the Savior's atonement, we could never have become cleansed from sin. We would have been unclean spirits throughout all eternity—precisely what Satan is (2 Nephi 9:12–13). That is why Alma taught, "It is expedient that an atonement should be made; for according to the great plan of the Eternal God there must be an atonement made, or else all mankind must unavoidably perish" (Alma 34:9). Little wonder Nephi cried out: "O the wisdom of God, his mercy and grace! . . . O how great the goodness of our God, who prepareth a way for our escape from the grasp of this awful monster; yea, that monster, death and hell, which I call the death of the body, and also the death of the spirit. . . . O how great the plan of our God!" (2 Nephi 9:8, 10, 13).

All that Christ passed through for us in his final hours will one day cause every knee to bow and every tongue to thank him for the Atonement and to thank Heavenly Father for the great plan of salvation.

NEVER GIVE UP

Because Christ paid the ultimate price for each of us, he will never cease trying to help us. It grieves him to lose any of us (Jacob 5:7, 11). He nourishes and strengthens us with his words (Jacob 5:12). He labors daily to touch our hearts (Jacob 5:16). He calls servants (prophets) to labor diligently with their might and invites others to join with them to help us (Jacob 5:61, 70). He promises all who help that they will have joy with him (Jacob 5:71, 75). He includes us in his work and in the rewards the Father will give him (Jacob 5:75; Mosiah 14:12). He never gives up trying to bless us, and he never gives up on us (Jacob 6:4).

He also expects us not to give up on ourselves and has counseled us not to give up on one another. That means children who stray, friends who fail, or loved ones who wander away from covenants: "Ye shall not cast him out of your synagogues, or your places of worship, for unto such shall ye continue to minister; for ye know not but what they will return and repent, and come unto me with full purpose of heart, and I shall heal them; and ye shall be the means of bringing salvation unto them" (3 Nephi 18:32). Elder Neal A. Maxwell reminds us, "Quickly forgotten by those who are offended is the fact that the Church is 'for the perfecting of the saints' (Eph. 4:12); it is not a well-provisioned rest home for the already perfected."[11]

At baptism we covenant to be willing to "bear one another's burdens, that they may be light" (Mosiah 18:8). The parable of the good Samaritan illustrates how. In the parable, a man leaves Jerusalem (as the holy city, or the high place, it is a type of heaven). He journeys down through dangerous terrain towards Jericho (the lowest place on earth, thirteen hundred feet below sea level). En route he is wounded: he needs help, or he will die. Those who claim to have authority cannot or will not help him. Finally, a good Samaritan (a type of Christ, who grew up near Samaria) has compassion on the man, pours oil over him to heal the wounds, binds them up, and carries the suffering traveler to an inn (a type of the Church of Christ). He promises the innkeeper he will return to pay him well for caring for the wounded individual (Luke 10:30–35).

The parallels between the man in the story and our own journey through mortality are striking.[12] We left heaven and are traveling down through dangerous terrain. We have lost everything and will die if we do not get help. The Savior can heal us, carry us, and take us to the inn, where he promises others great rewards if they will care for us until he returns. In one sense, we are the wounded individual who needs help. In another sense, we are the donkey the good Samaritan used to carry the wounded individual to the inn. And in still another sense, we are the innkeeper, charged with the responsibility to "succor the weak, lift up the hands which hang down, and strengthen the feeble knees" (D&C 81:5) until Christ returns again. We are our brothers' keepers (Moses 5:34).

The prophet Brigham Young had a vision that taught him the importance of never giving up on people. He was struggling with some of the Saints who wanted to abandon the work of establishing Zion in the Salt Lake Valley and move to California, where gold had been discovered. He spoke strongly in several meetings to persuade the Saints not to leave, not to forsake their responsibilities. One night, while pondering the situation, President Young had a dream, which he later shared. He said that in his dream he was going to get some goats he had purchased from another man:

"I looked up towards the road on my right, and behold I saw brother Joseph returning, riding on a waggon . . . as though he had been on a journey of some length. He alighted from the waggon, and came to where we were standing. I looked, and saw, following the waggon, an almost innumerable flock of sheep of all kinds, sizes, colours, and descriptions, from the largest, finest sheep I ever saw, down to the ugly decrepit dwarf. The wool on the large ones, I thought, was as white as snow; then the next smaller ones had also nice fine wool on them, and some were black and white; others had coarse long wool upon them, approximating to hair; and so on, until they became a mixture of goats and sheep. I looked on the strange flock and wondered. While I was looking, I asked Joseph what in the world he was going to do with such a flock of sheep, and said to him,

'Why, brother Joseph, you have the most singular flock of sheep I ever saw: what are you going to do with them?' He looked up and smiled, as he did when he was living, and as though he was in reality with me, and said, 'They are all good in their place.' This is the dream.

"So it is with this people. If you can only find the place for the goats, they answer the end for which they were made. I have always realized that a half-hearted 'Mormon' is one of the meanest of human beings, for such are always ready to say, 'How do you do, brother Devil?' and 'How do you do, brother Jesus?' or, 'Brother Jesus, I want to make you acquainted with brother Devil.' It is no trouble for them to turn unto Baal or unto Jesus; yet, at the same time, the Lord has a use for them. I have often heard men say they were convinced that 'Mormonism' was true, and that they would cleave to it; but as for their hearts being converted, it is altogether another thing. Mobs never have done one thing against this people, but they could trace them, and have known all about it; for you will always find that the goats will run and lick salt with the sheep; and the Lord who made them has placed them in the world to serve his own purpose."[13]

All people "are good in their place." But imagine how many more lives could be touched if we were more committed to Christ. Prophets, who are filled with the love of Christ, implore us to recognize the worth of souls and never to give up on others or on ourselves, especially "while his arm of mercy is extended towards [us] in the light of the day" (Jacob 6:5).

The atonement provided by Christ is a sure hope for eternal life: "Wherefore, whoso believeth in God might with surety hope [expect] for a better world, yea, even a place at the right hand of God, which hope [expectation] cometh of faith, maketh an anchor to the souls of men, which would make them sure and steadfast, always abounding in good works, being led to glorify God" (Ether 12:4).

Christ is the central figure in all history. He is the centerpiece in God's plan for our salvation. His final hours are important to every one of us. They began with his triumphal entry into Jerusalem almost two thousand years ago.

NOTES

1. Maxwell, Conference Report, April 1976, 39.
2. McConkie, *Mormon Doctrine,* 60.
3. LDS Bible Dictionary, s.v. "grace," 697.
4. Matthews, *A Bible!* 271.
5. Smith, *Teachings of the Prophet Joseph Smith,* 324.
6. Ibid., 181.
7. Smith, *Gospel Doctrine,* 442; Smith, *Journal of Discourses,* 19:264.
8. Widtsoe, "Worth of Souls," 189–90.
9. Hinckley, "Reach Out in Love and Kindness," 77.
10. Smith, *Gospel Doctrine,* 442; Smith, *Journal of Discourses,* 19:264.
11. Maxwell, "'Brother Offended,'" 38.
12. Welch, "Good Samaritan," 50–116.
13. Young, *Journal of Discourses,* 6:320–21.

TRIUMPHAL ENTRY

Blessed is he that cometh in the name of the Lord.
—Matthew 21:9

From an eternal perspective, nothing in life is more interesting to study again and again than the life, labors, and love of our Savior. The Savior's labor of love to give us new life began long before his mortal birth. Even from our premortal state, Jesus has had only one motive—to do his Father's will. Throughout his entire premortal, mortal, and postmortal life, Jesus has had the self-discipline to stay focused on the thing that really mattered most. Among the first recorded words from Jesus in the premortal life are, "Father, thy will be done, and the glory be thine forever" (Moses 4:2). The first recorded words from his mortal life are, "I must be about my Father's business" (Luke 2:49). The last words he spoke from the cross were, "Father, it is finished, thy will is done" (JST Matthew 27:54). Never has any father had such a devoted son. Little wonder that every time the Father appears on this earth his first statement is, "This is my beloved Son, in whom I am well pleased. Hear ye him" (JST Matthew 3:46). During his final hours, the Savior was completely focused on doing the Father's will. It was as if the Father were there himself.

THE FINAL WEEK

The final week of the Savior's life began in Bethany (map, page xii, location 1), which was home to Mary, Martha, and Lazarus. Jesus stayed in their home each night, and each day he went from there to the temple in Jerusalem and back. He would walk up and over the Mount of Olives (2), down the other side, and then up the Kidron Valley (4) to reach the temple in Jerusalem (6). The Kidron Valley lies on the eastern boundary of the city of Jerusalem. In King Josiah's time the southern end of the Kidron Valley was a cemetery (Jeremiah 26:23). Connecting with the Kidron Valley is the Hinnom Valley, where King Ahaz and idolatrous Jews offered children to Molech, god of fire (2 Chronicles 28:3; 33:6; Jeremiah 7:31; 19:2–6).[1] It later became a place where garbage was burned and was named Gehenna to symbolize the place of everlasting punishment.[2]

Each day of the last week of his life, the Savior would have walked down through Gethsemane (map, page xii, location 3), into the Kidron Valley (4), and then up to his Father's house, the temple (6). This walk foreshadowed the spiritual path he would tread in his final hours. It was a prefiguring of his descent through Gethsemane's agony down into death and the spirit world and then back up again into the presence of the Father.

As Jesus began his triumphal entry into Jerusalem, he looked up at the magnificent temple and wept. Three years earlier, when he began his ministry, he had referred to the temple as "my Father's house" and cleaned out the moneychangers (John 2:13–17). As he cleansed it a second time in his final week, he called the temple "my house" (Matthew 21:13). Finally, at the end of the week, he said, "Your house is left unto you desolate" (Matthew 23:38; emphasis added). It grieved the Savior to think that the people he had lived with and whom he loved greatly would not receive the blessings of the temple until after his second coming in the latter days. The living water flowing from the temple can give life and heal all who are dead to the things of the Spirit (Ezekiel 47:1–9).

With great compassion for them, he cried out: "O Jerusalem! Jerusalem! Ye who will kill the prophets, and will stone them who are sent unto you; how often would I have gathered your children together, even as a hen gathers her chickens under her wings, and ye would not! Behold, your house is left unto you desolate. For I say unto you, that ye shall not see me henceforth, and know that I am he of whom it is written by the prophets, until ye shall say, Blessed is he who cometh in the name of the Lord, in the clouds of heaven, and all the holy angels with him. Then understood his disciples that he should come again on the earth, after that he was glorified and crowned on the right hand of God" (JST Matthew 23:37–41).

One entrance into the temple courtyard was the Golden Gate (map, page xii, location 5). It lies a short distance north of the present Dome of the Rock. On Palm Sunday, the Sunday before his atoning sacrifice, the Savior made his triumphal entry through that gate.[3]

As a direct descendant of King David, Christ was legal heir to the throne in Israel. Had the Jews, rather than Rome, been governing Judea, Jesus would have indeed been the king of the Jews. In contrast to the Caesars who came to conquer Jerusalem, Jesus, the rightful heir, entered the city in peace to bless the people. The Prince of Peace made his official entry into Jerusalem in meekness, riding a donkey (Matthew 21:1–11), a symbol both of humility and of a king coming in peace to his coronation (1 Kings 1:33, 44).

As Christ entered the temple courtyard through the Golden Gate, he was greeted with the waving of palm branches and the Hosanna Shout (Matthew 21:6–9), both symbols of the Feast of Tabernacles, in which Jehovah was acknowledged as King of Israel.[4] The multitudes cried out, "Hosanna to the Son of David: Blessed is he that cometh in the name of the Lord; Hosanna in the highest" (Matthew 21:9).

Many of the Jews recognized him as their long-awaited Messiah. The word *hosanna* means "save us now."[5] The title "Son of David" was a sacred title reserved for the descendant of King David who would redeem them from their enemies.[6] Their long-anticipated day of deliverance was finally at hand.

His disciples walked beside him, loudly proclaiming, "Blessed be the King that cometh in the name of the Lord: peace in heaven, and glory in the highest" (Luke 19:38). Several self-righteous Pharisees who overheard them called on him to rebuke his disciples (Luke 19:37–39). He answered, "I tell you that, if these should hold their peace, the stones would immediately cry out" (Luke 19:40). If no one else would bear record of him at this triumphant entry, the very earth itself would.

As the Savior neared the city and saw the excitement of the crowds, he prayed: "Father, save me from this hour: but for this cause came I unto this hour. Father, glorify thy name." A voice answered him from heaven: "I have both glorified it, and will glorify it again" (John 12:27–28). Some thought an angel had spoken to him; others thought it was thunder. The Savior told them, "This voice came not because of me, but for your sakes. Now is the judgment of this world: now shall the prince of this world be cast out. And I, if I be lifted up from the earth, will draw all men unto me" (John 12:30–32).

The Jewish people expected the Messiah to lead the armies of Israel to victory and then establish a reign of peace and righteousness. They were anxious for that to happen. But, unfortunately, they looked beyond the mark, expecting him to do at his first coming some of the things he will do at his second coming. Instead of over-throwing Rome, Jesus declared, "Render therefore unto Caesar the things which are Caesar's; and unto God the things that are God's" (Matthew 22:21) and said, "My kingdom is not of this world" (John 18:36).

It is tragic that within the week some of the same voices that were shouting, "Hosanna to the Son of David," would cry out, "Crucify him, crucify him!" (Luke 23:21). But their rejection of him was caused by more than a misunderstanding of prophecy. The Joseph Smith Translation of the Bible makes it abundantly clear that per-sonal transgression and failure to heed the call to repent was at the heart of their treachery (see JST Matthew 3:34–36; JST Luke 14:35–37; JST Matthew 21:32–34; JST Matthew 23:24).

Even so, Christ's triumphal entry into the temple courtyard was a type of the triumphal entry he will make at the Second Coming. Before that glorious second advent, latter-day disciples will have proclaimed his coming with loud voices. With great anticipation a reverential hush will settle over the whole earth (Revelation 8:1; D&C 88:95). Then, suddenly, he will come. The earth and the stones will cry out as thunder, lightning, and quakes accompany his appearance (D&C 88:89–90). Arrayed in bright red robes he will descend to earth with the sound of trumpets and the shout of the hosts of heaven (Isaiah 63:1; Revelation 19:13; D&C 133:48). On his vesture will be written the title, "KING OF KINGS, AND LORD OF LORDS" (JST Revelation 19:16). At the time of this second triumphal entry, those living in Jerusalem will realize that Christ is the very same person who entered Jerusalem triumphantly so long ago. "And then shall they weep because of their iniquities; then shall they lament because they persecuted their king" (D&C 45:53).

THE EVENTS OF THE FINAL WEEK

Beginning with his first triumphal entry into Jerusalem, Christ entered the temple daily to teach the people and then returned to Bethany each evening to be alone with his disciples. During his final week, he did the following:

Cursed hypocrisy (Matthew 23:27–28) and chastised hypocrites (Matthew 22:18; 23:13).

Cleansed the temple for the second time because they had "trample[d him] under their feet" (1 Nephi 19:7) by making sacred celebrations and sacred places into circuslike events. Holy days had become holidays, and there was no longer any room for him.

Taught the common people who were "very attentive to hear him" and who "heard him gladly" but condemned "the chief priests and the scribes and the chief of the people" who were "offended at him" and who "sought to destroy him" (JST Mark 12:44; Luke 19:47–48).

Answered hard questions (questions asked with hardened spirits) with his own questions. He discerned that the religious leaders would answer him only out of their fears of the multitude because they were more worried about their positions of authority with the people than they were about knowing the truth (Matthew 21:25–27; JST Matthew 21:47–49).

Taught at the temple daily. He taught the people about his role in the Father's plan for his children: "For he [God] hath sent him [Christ] among you that ye might have life" (JST Matthew 23:7).

Sternly rebuked the Jewish rulers in three parables because they had failed as custodians over the kingdom of God (the parables of the two sons, the wicked husbandmen, and the royal marriage; Matthew 21:28–46; 22:1–14). He also spoke plainly about their transgressions and taught the people not to follow the Jewish leaders' hypocritical behavior (JST Matthew 23:1–2).

Bore witness of the resurrection (Matthew 22:29–33).

Taught which of all the commandments is the greatest to keep (Matthew 22:35–40).

Reminded the people of the many prophets who had been sent to Jerusalem and how often they had been rejected: "Behold your fathers did it through ignorance, but ye do not; wherefore, their sins shall be upon your heads" (JST Matthew 23:35). He also foretold that destruction would come upon Jerusalem and that the temple would be so thoroughly destroyed that "there shall not be left here one stone upon another" (Matthew 24:2).

Taught the people what they needed to do to be spared the prophesied destruction (Joseph Smith–Matthew 1:1–19).

Blessed the disciples in the temple (JST Mark 11:13) and taught them that those who would reject him in that day would be broken, "and the kingdom of God shall be taken from them" (JST Matthew 21:52). He also taught that the kingdom of God would be given to the Gentiles in the latter days (JST Matthew 21:53–56). In these verses the Joseph Smith Translation "emphasizes that Jesus' testimony of himself to his disciples during the last week of his mortal ministry was more clear, sure, and powerful than the King James Version portrays."[7]

Met with the Twelve Apostles privately to teach them more about the destruction of Jerusalem and about his second coming in the latter days (Joseph Smith–Matthew).

Taught his disciples what they must do to prepare for the Second Coming (Matthew 25). "What I say unto one, I say unto all, Watch ye therefore, and pray always, and keep my commandments, that ye may be counted worthy to escape all these things which shall come to pass, and to stand before the Son of man when he shall come clothed in the glory of his Father" (JST Luke 21:36).

At the end of this very busy and challenging week, Christ called the apostles together for the Last Supper, the final Passover.

NOTES

1. LDS Bible Dictionary, s.v. "Molech," 733.
2. Ibid., s.v. "Gehenna," 678.
3. That is the traditional view. For a contrasting opinion, see Murphy-O'Connor, *Holy Land,* 93–94.
4. McConkie, *Promised Messiah,* 433–34.
5. LDS Bible Dictionary, s.v. "Hosanna," 704–5.
6. Ludlow, "Greatest Week in History," 35.
7. Skinner, "Restored Light," 18.

THE LAST SUPPER

Then came the day of unleavened bread, when the passover must be killed.
—Luke 22:7

The Feast of the Passover was instituted to help the children of Israel remember when the destroying angel passed over Israel and delivered them from Egypt (Exodus 12:21–28). Only those homes marked with the blood of a lamb were spared. The week-long Passover in the Savior's day was a freedom festival celebrating Israel's deliverance by Jehovah, which culminated with a family dinner. Sometime on Thursday afternoon of the final week of the Savior's life, in the Court of the Priests at the temple, the blood of sacrificial lambs flowed freely. They were sacrificed in commemoration of the first Passover but also in anticipation of the ultimate Passover, when the Lamb of God would be slain. At the very hour that lambs were being offered up, Jesus began submitting to the requirements of the Atonement.

The Last Supper was held in a "guestchamber . . . a large upper room" belonging to one of his disciples (Mark 14:14–15).[1] The traditional site of the Last Supper lies in the southwestern part of

Jerusalem (map, page xii, location 7). Christ instructed Peter and John to prepare the Passover so they could eat:

"And they said unto him, Where wilt thou that we prepare?" (Luke 22:9).

"And he said unto them, Behold, when ye have entered into the city, there shall a man meet you bearing a pitcher of water; follow him into the house where he entereth in. And ye shall say unto the good man of the house, The Master saith unto you, Where is the guest-chamber, where I shall eat the passover with my disciples?" (JST Luke 22:10–11).

"And he shall shew you a large upper room furnished: there make ready. And they went, and found as he had said unto them: and they made ready the passover. And when the hour was come, he sat down, and the twelve apostles with him" (Luke 22:12–14).

There were obviously some great revelations here. The owner of the home was inspired to make everything ready. Peter and John were also led by the Spirit of revelation to find the right man at a time when Jerusalem was very busy and very crowded. Usually a woman carried the water from the well to the home, but in this case, a man was serving the family. He was a disciple of Christ who owned a large "guest-chamber," where this unique and climactic Seder meal was now ready and waiting.

The word *seder* means "ordered, arranged, prepared." It involved the right foods, the right prayers, and specific sayings repeated together. All the foods, the sayings, and the prayers pointed to Jesus Christ. It must have been incredibly meaningful for Peter and John, the presiding officers of the Church, to be chosen to make ready the last symbolic sacrifice preparatory for Christ's offering, the only real sacrifice that could save mankind from sin.

"THE GREATEST AMONG YOU"

Lying on the table was the roast lamb, symbolizing the Savior who would himself be sacrificed that night. The Lamb of God must have had some soul-stirring thoughts as he looked at the sacrificial lamb lying there, knowing full well that for the last four millennia it had been a type of what was to happen to him this night.

At the table a disagreement arose about which one of the apostles was the greatest (Luke 22:24–30). Judas, already filled with an evil spirit, may have started the strife.[2]

Christ was the greatest of all those in the room, yet they were perhaps arguing about which one of them should be seated at the head of the table. He could have thundered reminders of how important he and the events of this particular night were. Instead, he showed great humility, as he had earlier in his ministry when he taught the Twelve: "If any man desire to be first, he shall be last of all, and servant of all. And he took a child, and sat in the midst of them; and when he had taken the child in his arms, he said unto them, Whosoever shall humble himself like one of these children, and receiveth me, ye shall receive in my name. And whosoever shall receive me, receiveth not me only, but him that sent me, even the Father" (JST Mark 9:32–35).

On this night of nights, he set a perfect example of the principle he had taught by washing the apostles' feet, and he asked them to continue to perform this ordinance for each other. As the ultimate ordinance of condemnation is to "shake off the dust of your feet" (Matthew 10:14; D&C 24:15), so the ultimate ordinance of acceptance by Christ is the washing of the feet: "Ye call me Master and Lord; and ye say well; for so I am. If I then, your Lord and Master, have washed your feet; ye also ought to wash one another's feet. For I have given you an example, that ye should do as I have done to you. Verily, verily, I say unto you, The servant is not greater than his lord; neither he that is sent greater than he that sent him. If ye know these things, happy are ye if ye do them" (John 13:13–17).

There was no display of ego here. True humility seeks to bless others with no self-promotion involved. Christ humbly showed us that the greatest among us is the servant of all (Matthew 23:11).

The sound of the water being poured into a basin as he began to wash his disciples' feet reminds us all that we ought to serve one another. One author wrote: "When I am tempted to listen to hot, egotistic voices within my own heart; when it seems that love can never win but always loses; when it seem as though humility is ruthlessly trodden down by those who pass over it on their way to their own selfish ambitions; when it seems as though God cannot possibly triumph; when pity and love and mercy and kindness and tenderness are weakness; when it seems as though greatness is only possessed by those who know how to grab, and have the power to snatch at it, no matter what the cost to others—ah, yes, when voices sound in my own heart which say you must play for your own hand, you must think of number one, you must not let yourself be trodden down—when I am thus tempted, my God! may I hear in imagination the tinkling of water, poured into a basin, and see, as in a vision, the Son of God, washing the disciples' feet."[3]

President Harold B. Lee, almost two thousand years after the Last Supper took place, was taught this same principle by the Master Teacher. Just before the dedication of the Los Angeles California Temple, President Lee was busily preparing for that event and had an experience that he later shared in general conference: "Along about three or four o'clock in the morning, I enjoyed an experience that I think was not a dream, but it must have been a vision. It seemed that I was witnessing a great spiritual gathering, where men and women were standing up, two or three at a time, and speaking in tongues. The spirit was so unusual. I seemed to have heard the voice of President David O. McKay say, 'If you want to love God, you have to learn to love and serve the people. That is the way you show your love for God.'"[4]

"LORD, IS IT I?"

At some point during the Passover feast Jesus was "troubled in spirit" and made a startling announcement: "Verily, verily, I say unto you, that one of you shall betray me. Then the disciples looked one on another, doubting of whom he spake" (John 13:21–22).

As the meal progressed, they all asked him, one by one, "Lord, is it I?" (Matthew 26:22). When Judas asked, the Savior replied, "Thou hast said" (Matthew 26:25). The Joseph Smith Translation makes it clear that Judas "acted out of rebellion and ignored an ultimate warning from the Messiah himself."[5] "And he [Jesus] said unto Judas Iscariot, What thou doest, do quickly; but beware of innocent blood.

Nevertheless, Judas Iscariot, even one of the twelve, went unto the chief priests to betray Jesus unto them; for he turned away from him, and was offended because of his words" (JST Mark 14:30–31).

Have you ever wondered why the others didn't stop Judas or at least say something to him? One reason could be the way they were seated. Most Christian artists paint the Last Supper with the Savior and disciples seated upright at a large table. But tables in the Middle East were, as they still are in many places today, low to the ground. Those around the table reclined, leaning on one arm with their feet pointing away from the table, or sat cross-legged at the table. Judas was apparently seated to the left of Christ and could have asked him very quietly without others hearing while the feast was in progress. John the Beloved was seated on the Savior's right. Peter, being seated across the table, motioned to John and asked him to find out who would betray their Lord:

"Now there was leaning on Jesus' bosom one of his disciples [John], whom Jesus loved. Simon Peter therefore beckoned to him, that he should ask who it should be of whom he spake. He then lying on Jesus' breast saith unto him, Lord, who is it? Jesus answered, He it is, to whom I shall give a sop, when I have dipped it. And when he had dipped the sop, he gave it to Judas Iscariot, the son of Simon. And after the sop Satan entered into him. Then said Jesus unto him, That thou doest, do quickly" (John 13:23–27).

Apparently, before John could say anything to Peter, Judas got up and left the room. "Now no man at the table knew for what intent he [Jesus] spake this unto him [Judas]. For some of them thought, because Judas had the bag, that Jesus had said unto him, Buy those things that we have need of against the feast; or, that he should give something to the poor. He then having received the sop went immediately out: and it was night" (John 13:28–30).

They assumed Judas had gone to buy bread. They did not realize he was going out to betray the Bread of Life into the hands of wicked men. Judas went to the palace of Caiaphas (map, page xii, location 8) to get a band of men. Ironically, Judas was later that night rejected and betrayed by those who conspired with him to betray Jesus. The Joseph Smith Translation makes it clear that he did not act in ignorance.

Judas totally understood the Savior's warning and willfully rebelled against him (JST Matthew 27:3–6).

"PEACE I LEAVE WITH YOU"

Sometimes great spiritual experiences can come only after the wicked are gone, as when Nephi had to leave his brothers outside the city wall before the Spirit could lead him (1 Nephi 4:5–6), or as will be the case when the earth experiences the millennial day of peace after the wicked have been destroyed. Once Judas was gone, the Savior gave his greatest teachings. He told the apostles of the events soon to take place. He taught about the celestial law of love and reminded his disciples that he was about to leave them but promised he would not leave them comfortless. He would send "the Comforter," the Holy Ghost, who would "bring all things to your remembrance, whatsoever I have said unto you" (John 14:26).

This was a marvelous gift. "The greatest gift known to and enjoyed by mortals," Elder Bruce R. McConkie said, "is the gift of the Holy Ghost, which is the right to the constant companionship of that member of the Godhead based on righteousness."[6] The Prophet Joseph Smith instructed Brigham Young to teach the Saints about the important blessings bestowed by the Holy Ghost. "The Spirit of the Lord," he said, "will whisper peace and joy to their souls; it will take malice, hatred, strife and all evil from their hearts; and their whole desire will be to do good, bring forth righteousness and build up the kingdom of God. . . . If they will follow the spirit of the Lord they will go right."[7]

Christ also promised his apostles a second comforter: "I will pray the Father, and he shall give you another Comforter, that he may abide with you forever" (John 14:16).

Who is this other comforter? The Prophet Joseph Smith gives us the answer: "It is no more nor less than the Lord Jesus Christ Himself. . . . When any man obtains this last Comforter, he will have the personage of Jesus Christ to attend him or appear unto him from time to time, and even He will manifest the Father unto him, and they will take up their abode with him, and the visions of the heavens will be opened unto him, and the Lord will teach him face to face, and he may have a perfect knowledge of the mysteries of the Kingdom of God; and this is the state and place the ancient Saints arrived at when they had such glorious visions."[8]

Knowing that trials and afflictions awaited them, the Savior blessed his disciples: "Peace I leave with you, my peace I give unto you: not as the world giveth, give I unto you. Let not your heart be troubled, neither let it be afraid" (John 14:27).

He has promised similar rewards for our placing our trust in him (D&C 93:1). Even when we do not understand the purpose of a trial or commandment, we can be confident that following God will always be to our benefit and blessing: "Verily, verily, I say unto thee, put your trust in that Spirit which leadeth to do good—yea, to do justly, to walk humbly, to judge righteously; and this is my Spirit. Verily, verily, I say unto you, I will impart unto you of my Spirit, which shall enlighten your mind, which shall fill your soul with joy; and then shall ye know, or by this shall you know, all things whatsoever you desire of me, which are pertaining unto things of righteousness, in faith believing in me that you shall receive" (D&C 11:12–14).

President Ezra Taft Benson taught: "Though persecutions arise, though reverses come, in prayer we can find reassurance, for God will speak peace to the soul. That peace, that spirit of serenity, is life's greatest blessing."[9]

The Savior instructed his disciples at the Last Supper always to draw strength from the true Source of Life: "I am the true vine, and my Father is the husbandman. . . . I am the vine, ye are the branches: he that abideth in me, and I in him, the same bringeth forth much fruit" (John 15:1–5). He promised them that he would be resurrected (John 16:16) and that their sorrow at his death would be "turned into joy" (John 16:20). "These things I have spoken unto you," he said, "that in me ye might have peace. In the world ye shall have tribulation: but be of good cheer; I have overcome the world" (John 16:33). Knowing that Christ has overcome the world brings us peace and enables us to be of good cheer in times of tribulation, sorrow, and disappointment.

Christ then prayed for his disciples and offered the High Priestly Prayer. Once a year at Passover, the high priest would enter the Holy of Holies in the temple and offer an intercessory prayer, meaning that he stood between Israel and God to plead for their salvation. Christ is the great High Priest, who now poured out his soul for our salvation: "Father, the hour is come; glorify thy Son, that thy Son also may glorify thee: As thou hast given him power over all flesh, that he should give eternal life to as many as thou hast given him. And this is life eternal, that they might know thee the only true God, and Jesus Christ, whom thou hast sent" (John 17:1–3).

In a revelation given to the Prophet Joseph Smith, the Savior shared another intercessory prayer describing his role as our advocate with the Father. He pleads on our behalf: "Father, behold the sufferings and death of him who did no sin, in whom thou wast well pleased; behold the blood of thy Son which was shed, the blood of him whom thou gavest that thyself might be glorified; wherefore, Father, spare these my brethren that believe on my name, that they may come unto me and have everlasting life. Hearken, O ye people of my church, and ye elders listen together. . . . I came unto mine own, and mine own received me not; but unto as many as received me gave I power to do many miracles, and to become the sons of God; and even unto them that believed on my name gave I power to obtain eternal life" (D&C 45:4–8).

At some point during the Passover meal the Savior counseled Peter, "When thou art converted, strengthen thy brethren" (Luke 22:32). To have a testimony is to know, to testify. But to be converted is to do, to become. True conversion is commitment, as President Ezra Taft Benson noted: "A testimony of Jesus means that you accept the divine mission of Jesus Christ, embrace His gospel, and do His works."[10] Peter took the Savior's admonition to heart and later became one of the "doers of the word" and a great witness for Christ in the early Christian era (James 1:22).

Another instruction was given by the Savior to his apostles: "A new commandment I give unto you, That ye love one another; as I have loved you, that ye also love one another. By this shall all men know that ye are my disciples, if ye have love one to another" (John 13:34–35).

The old commandment was "thou shalt love thy neighbour as

thyself" (Leviticus 19:18). Sometimes we fail to love our neighbors because we don't know how to love ourselves. If we love ourselves too much, for example, we become self-absorbed and fail to show love for others. If we love ourselves too little, we become self-disdaining and lack the capacity to show love to others. But now a higher law of love was introduced. By raising the standard to this new level, everything changed. The focus was now on Christ's love, not ours. We are to love each other as he loves us, not as we love ourselves. In heaven everything is motivated by pure, godly love for others. Here on earth we often withhold our love and deal it out as if there were only a limited supply. Gratefully, the Savior's love is not contracted, and because of his new commandment, neither should ours be.

THE SACRAMENT OF THE LORD'S SUPPER INTRODUCED

During the Seder service the Savior turned the Passover feast into a sacramental meal (Luke 22:1–20), thus bridging the sacrifices of the old covenant with his "great and last sacrifice" of the new covenant (Alma 34:10).

Elder Bruce R. McConkie noted how closely the Passover and the sacrament of the Lord's Supper were linked: "As animal sacrifice was done away the sacrament was introduced. . . . And indeed, so united was their joint witness that the very rituals and performances of the last Paschal Supper were used to form the rituals and performances of the first sacrament of the Lord's Supper. The Paschal meal in Jesus' day called for the devout worshippers to bless both bread and wine and to eat and drink. Jesus simply took the symbols of the past and gave them a new meaning for the future."[11]

The Last Supper is called last because it was the last supper Jesus had as a mortal and, more important, because it was the final Passover to be recognized by God. A new ordinance had been introduced to take its place. And just as the Passover had pointed hearts and minds forward to the "great and last sacrifice" for the preceding four millennia (Alma 34:10), so the emblems of the sacrament would now point hearts and minds back to the events that occurred that night. The Passover signified deliverance from death; the sacrament signified new life (Mark 14:22–25). Truly the "hopes and fears of all the years" were met in him that night at the last Passover and the first sacrament of the Lamb of God.[12]

The sacrament was instituted during that part of the Seder meal when the matzoh, or unleavened bread, was broken and eaten.[13] Some Seder meals use three pieces of matzoh covered with a napkin. The middle piece of bread is removed and broken in pieces, an unmistakable type of Christ, the second member of the Godhead, whose body was broken and then covered with a burial shroud.

The Gospels record the Savior's words as follows: "And as they did eat, Jesus took bread and blessed it, and brake, and gave to them, and said, Take it, and eat. Behold, this is for you to do in remembrance of my body [JST Matthew 26:22 adds "which I give a ransom for you"]; for as oft as ye do this ye will remember this hour that I was with you" (JST Mark 14:20–21).

The wine at Passover is red in color, like the blood of the lambs that was smeared on the doorposts at the first Passover. It reminds us of the blood Christ shed to redeem us and save us from death: "And he took the cup, and gave thanks, and gave it to them, saying, Drink ye all of it. For this is in remembrance of my blood . . . which is shed for as many as shall believe on my name, for the remission of their sins" (JST Matthew 26:23–24). For some the emblems of the sacrament might seem little more than a crust of bread and a sip of water. But for those who come with broken hearts and contrite spirits, who come seeking forgiveness of sin, the emblems become manna sent from heaven, the Bread of Life, the assurance and hope for new life (John 6:33, 35) and a well of water springing up to eternal life (John 4:14).

As they were participating in the new ordinance, the Savior foretold a future sacrament meeting: "I say unto you, I will not drink henceforth of this fruit of the vine, until that day when I drink it new with you in my Father's kingdom" (Matthew 26:29). From modern revelation we know that statement refers to a future sacrament meeting in a great priesthood gathering (D&C 27).[14]

CONCLUDING THE SEDER

As their Passover concluded, the Savior commanded the apostles to "bear record [of him] unto all the world" (JST Mark 14:23) and announced that this would be their last meeting together. "They were grieved" and at hearing this "wept over him" (JST Mark 14:26). The Savior then told Peter he would deny Him three times that night (Matthew 26:33–34).

Finally, they sang a hymn. Sacred music brings spiritual strength. By so doing, Christ taught us how to prepare for difficulties that lie ahead in life. Like prayer, sacred music lifts our souls to greater heights and places our spirits in greater harmony with God: "For my soul delighteth in the song of the heart; yea, the song of the righteous is a prayer unto me, and it shall be answered with a blessing upon their heads" (D&C 25:12).

If this Passover meal was typical of the meals that had been held since King David's day, the song they would have sung is the Hallel (meaning "hallelujah"*)*. The messianic verses all point to Jesus Christ and his sacrifice. We are not certain if this was what they sang, but the Hallel is found in Psalms 113 through 118 and contains many phrases that have reference to Christ's atoning sacrifice, such as the following:

"Praise ye the Lord. Praise, O ye servants of the Lord, praise the name of the Lord.

"Blessed be the name of the Lord from this time forth and for evermore.

"From the rising of the sun unto the going down of the same the Lord's name is to be praised.

"The Lord is high above all nations, and his glory above the heavens.

"Who is like unto the Lord our God, who dwelleth on high,

"Who humbleth himself to behold the things that are in heaven, and in the earth!

"He raiseth up the poor out of the dust, and lifteth the needy out of the dunghill;

"That he may set him with princes, even with the princes of his people.

"He maketh the barren woman to keep house, and to be a joyful mother of children. Praise ye the Lord" (Psalm 113).

"When Israel went out of Egypt, the house of Jacob from a people of strange language;

"Judah was his sanctuary, and Israel his dominion.

"The sea saw it, and fled; Jordan was driven back.

"The mountains skipped like rams, and the little hills like lambs.

"What ailed thee, O thou sea, that thou fleddest? thou Jordan, that thou wast driven back?

"Ye mountains, that ye skipped like rams; and ye little hills, like lambs?

"Tremble, thou earth, at the presence of the Lord, at the presence of the God of Jacob;

"Which turned the rock into a standing water, the flint into a fountain of waters" (Psalm 114).

"Not unto us, O Lord, not unto us, but unto thy name be glory, for thy mercy, and for thy truth's sake. . . .

"O Israel, trust thou in the Lord; he is thy help and thy shield.

"O house of Aaron, trust in the Lord; he is thy help and thy shield.

"Ye that fear the Lord, trust in the Lord; he is your help and your shield (JST Psalm 115:1–11).

"The Lord hath been mindful of us: he will bless us; he will bless the house of Israel; he will bless the house of Aaron.

"He will bless them that fear the Lord, both small and great.

"The Lord shall increase you more and more, you and your children.

"Ye are blessed of the Lord which made heaven and earth.

"The heaven, even the heavens, are the Lord's: but the earth hath he given to the children of men. . . .

"But we will bless the Lord from this time forth and for evermore. Praise the Lord" (Psalm 115:12–18).

"I love the Lord, because he hath heard my voice and my supplications.

"Because he hath inclined his ear unto me, therefore will I call upon him as long as I live.

"The sorrows of death compassed me, and the pains of hell gat hold upon me: I found trouble and sorrow.

"Then called I upon the name of the Lord; O Lord, I beseech thee, deliver my soul.

"Gracious is the Lord, and righteous; yea, our God is merciful. . . .

"For thou hast delivered my soul from death, mine eyes from tears, and my feet from falling. . . .

"What shall I render unto the Lord for all his benefits toward me?

"I will take the cup of salvation, and call upon the name of the Lord.

"I will pay my vows unto the Lord now in the presence of all his people. . . .

"O Lord, truly I am thy servant; I am thy servant, and the son of thine handmaid: thou hast loosed my bonds" (Psalm 116:1–16).

"O praise the Lord, all ye nations: praise him, all ye people.

"For his merciful kindness is great toward us: and the truth of the Lord endureth for ever. Praise ye the Lord" (Psalm 117).

"O give thanks unto the Lord; for he is good: because his mercy endureth for ever.

"Let Israel now say, that his mercy endureth for ever.

"Let the house of Aaron now say, that his mercy endureth for ever.

"Let them now that fear the Lord say, that his mercy endureth for ever.

"I called upon the Lord in distress: the Lord answered me, and set me in a large place. . . .

"The Lord is my strength and song, and is become my salvation. . . .

"I shall not die, but live, and declare the works of the Lord.

"The Lord hath chastened me sore: but he hath not given me over unto death.

"Open to me the gates of righteousness: I will go into them, and I will praise the Lord:

"This gate of the Lord, into which the righteous shall enter.

"I will praise thee: for thou hast heard me, and art become my salvation.

"The stone which the builders refused is become the head stone of the corner.

"This is the Lord's doing; it is marvellous in our eyes.

"This is the day which the Lord hath made; we will rejoice and be glad in it.

"Save now, I beseech thee, O Lord: O Lord, I beseech thee, send now prosperity. . . .

"God is the Lord, which hath shewed us light: bind the sacrifice with cords, even unto the horns of the altar.

"Thou art my God, and I will praise thee: thou art my God, I will exalt thee.

"O give thanks unto the Lord; for he is good: for his mercy endureth for ever" (Psalm 118:1–29).

Everything had been perfectly prepared for this final Passover, and now, after the singing of a hymn, the Savior was prepared to make the offering of the ages. The angel of death that had spared the children of Israel at the first Passover would, on the morrow, receive the blood of life from the Redeemer. Just as the blood of all sacrificial offerings had been "poured out . . . at the bottom of the altar" (Leviticus 9:9) and spilled upon the earth (Moses 5:5), so the blood of the Lamb of God would now be poured out before God in the Garden of Gethsemane (Moses 5:7; Deuteronomy 12:27).

It was late at night when they finished the Last Supper. As their Passover closed, Christ bore his testimony to his beloved apostles: "And I tell you these things, that ye may know that I love the Father; and as the Father gave me commandment, even so I do. Arise, let us go hence" (JST John 14:31). Then "they went out into the mount of Olives" (JST Matthew 26:27) and made their way to Gethsemane.

NOTES

1. Elder Bruce R. McConkie suggested that John Mark's family provided the room for the Passover (*Mortal Messiah,* 4:23–24, 28).
2. McConkie, *Mortal Messiah,* 4:34.
3. Weatherhead, "When I Am Tempted," 741, as cited in *Christ's Ideals for Living,* 269.
4. Lee, "'Stand Ye in Holy Places,'" 124.
5. Skinner, "Restored Light," 19.
6. McConkie, *Mortal Messiah,* 4:96.
7. Watson, *Manuscript History of Brigham Young,* 529–30.
8. Smith, *Teachings of the Prophet Joseph Smith,* 150.
9. Benson, Conference Report, April 1977, 47.
10. Benson, Conference Report, April 1982, 89.

11. McConkie, *New Witness,* 295.

12. *Hymns,* no. 208.

13. Reynolds and Sjodahl, *Commentary on the Book of Mormon,* 4:370.

14. Smith, *Progress of Man,* 479–82; McConkie, *Millennial Messiah,* 586–87.

THE GARDEN
OF GETHSEMANE

5

Then cometh Jesus with them unto a place called Gethsemane.
—Matthew 26:36

The lunar calendar and the Jewish calendar help us determine that there was a full moon the night Christ entered the Garden of Gethsemane. If the night was clear, Jesus would have been able to see the temple across from the garden as well as a graveyard that lay on the southern end of the Mount of Olives. After this night, the grasp of the grave over mortals would be broken. Mankind would be forever free to return to God's temple—God's presence.

Christ's suffering for the sins of the world, which allowed men to find peace with God, was performed on the Mount of Olives in an olive vineyard (Luke 22:39). The olive tree is a symbol of peace (Genesis 8:11). Olive oil provided light for lamps. Pure olive oil is a type of Christ, "the Prince of Peace" (Isaiah 9:6), the "light of the world" (John 8:12).

The word *Gethsemane* comes from the Hebrew *gath,* "press," and *shemen,* "oil." Gethsemane was a small olive grove with an olive press. Olive oil, used for healing, nutrition, light, and anointing, was extracted when the olives were subjected to immense pressure. Here, in Gethsemane, the weight of all mortal sins—past, present, and future—pressed upon the perfect, sinless Messiah and the healing "balm of Gilead" was extracted from his soul.[1] His name, Jesus the Christ, refers to his role as the Anointed One, for he was anointed before he was born to be the redeemer of all mankind.[2] His atonement empowered him to pour oil over our wounds to heal us (Luke 10:34) and give us "the oil of joy for mourning" (Isaiah 61:3).

The process for extracting oil from olives is an instructive one. Ripened olives are harvested and placed in a circular trough. A large and very heavy stone is then rolled around and around, passing over the olives to break them up. At first the olives are bruised, then they are broken, and eventually the weight of the stone turns the olives into a gray-green mash from which oozes the oil. Sometimes the mash is transferred into burlap sacks and tied off tightly. The bags are placed on a second type of press, this one having a large stone attached to a lever. The stone is lowered onto the bags of olive mash, and immense pressure is applied by turning the lever. Soon the oil begins to ooze from the olives and out through the pores of the bag. The first thing to appear is a bright red juice, which is followed by the clear-colored olive oil.

In Gethsemane, this place of pressing, Jesus was pressed down by the weight of the sins and suffering of the world until his atoning blood, which provides us with healing, oozed from every pore (Matthew 26:36–37; Luke 22:44; D&C 19:18). "Surely he hath borne our griefs, and carried our sorrows. . . . He was wounded for our transgressions, he was bruised for our iniquities" (Isaiah 53:4–5). The olive trees in the Garden of Gethsemane today are gnarled and twisted, as if bearing witness of the agony that took place there for us.

THE FIRST AND SECOND BIRTHS COMPARED

The sacrifice of Christ, which provides second birth for all, has some significant spiritual parallels to the process of our first birth. Like the Atonement, childbirth is a miracle. The mother enters into a partnership with God in becoming the caretaker of a soul. It is a sacred experience, but it involves excruciating pain and travail (Micah 4:9; Galatians 4:19). The sacrifice involves the presence of the Spirit and the shedding of blood and water (Moses 6:58–60). "Just as a mother's body may be permanently marked with the signs of pregnancy and childbirth, [so the Savior] said, 'I have graven thee upon the palms of my hands.' (1 Nephi 21:15–16.) For both a mother and the Savior, those marks memorialize a wrenching sacrifice, the sacrifice of begetting life—for her, physical birth; for him, spiritual rebirth."[3] Everyone in mortality experiences the first birth. Everyone can experience a spiritual rebirth and must do so to enter the celestial kingdom (Mosiah 27:25–26).

THE DEMANDS OF JUSTICE

We might ask, Why did anyone have to suffer, especially the Savior? Why is there a punishment attached to sin? The scriptures explain that the law of eternal justice demands that no unclean thing dwell in the presence of God (Moses 6:57). If unclean beings were allowed to dwell where God is, heaven would cease to exist. "The kingdom of God is not filthy, and there cannot any unclean thing enter into the kingdom of God; wherefore there must needs be a place of filthiness prepared for that which is filthy" (1 Nephi 15:34).

Since we have all broken some law or commandment at one time or another, we are forever disqualified by the law of justice from dwelling in God's presence. That's why the apostle James said, "For whosoever shall keep the whole law, and yet offend in one point, he is guilty of all" (James 2:10). In other words, even if we break only one law of God, we are subject to the demands of the law of justice.

Justice requires that when a law is broken a penalty be paid. Justice makes no allowance for sin (D&C 1:31), much as a bank holding a mortgage on a home doesn't care who pays off the debt so long as the debt is paid. It is merciful that Christ's suffering gave him the power and ability necessary to pay all our debts in full.

Wickedness brings with it the demand from justice that the guilty be punished (Mosiah 7:30–31). Sometimes we tend to think of God as being the one who will punish us, when in reality he is trying to help us avoid having to suffer the eternal consequences of sin (Mosiah 7:33). It grieves the Lord to see us suffer (Moses 7:29, 37). When Alma was counseling with his wayward son, Corianton, he sensed that his son did not understand God's desire to help him. Because Corianton had committed a very serious sin, he assumed God was going to punish him. Corianton felt it was unjust for a sinner to be "consigned to a state of misery" (Alma 42:1). He was thinking God was the cause of his suffering, but in truth, wickedness never brings happiness (Alma 41:10; Helaman 13:38). Alma patiently explained to Corianton that the demands of the law of justice were headed towards him. He testified that God was willing to step between him and the demands of justice, if Corianton was willing to repent. God's only desire is to bless and save us. He offers to help us overcome our fallen condition, based on our repentance and willingness to do as he asks. Alma assured Corianton—and all of us—that Christ's atonement fully satisfies the demands of justice and can protect us from the punishments that otherwise are headed our way. Those who refuse to allow Him to pay the penalty will have to suffer even as Christ did:

"Therefore I command you to repent . . . [or] your sufferings be sore—how sore you know not, how exquisite you know not, yea, how hard to bear you know not.

"For behold, I, God, have suffered these things for all, that they might not suffer if they would repent;

"But if they would not repent they must suffer even as I;

"Which suffering caused myself, even God, the greatest of all, to tremble because of pain, and to bleed at every pore, and to suffer both body and spirit—and would that I might not drink the bitter cup. . . .

"Nevertheless, glory be to the Father, and I partook and finished my preparations unto the children of men" (D&C 19:15–19).

HANDLING TRIALS WITHOUT SELF-ABSORBING SELF-PITY

As the Savior approached the Garden of Gethsemane, where the "chastisement of our peace" would fall on him (Isaiah 53:5), both he and his disciples began to be "sore amazed" and "very heavy" (Mark 14:33), phrases used to translate Greek words that mean "astonished," "awestruck," "depressed," and "dejected." They were all feeling the oppressive gravity of the moment and were overwhelmed with sorrow. Even the Savior, whose bright mind and keen intellect is greater than ours, both individually and collectively (Abraham 3:19), was stunned at the intensity of the pain and agony pressing upon him. He was sinless, so he did not know what sin was like from experience. Now it had his full attention. "Imagine," Elder Neal A. Maxwell said, "Jehovah, the Creator of this and other worlds, 'astonished'! Jesus knew cognitively what He must do, but not experientially. He had never personally known the exquisite and exacting process of an atonement before. Thus, when the agony came in its fulness, it was so much, much worse than even He with his unique intellect had ever imagined!"[4] Yet, he who suffered the most showed no self-pity. In fact, he helped and served others throughout the ordeal despite his own agony.

THE DEPTH OF THE SAVIOR'S SUFFERING

When we picture the Atonement in the Garden of Gethsemane, we often think of Christ kneeling in prayer beside a rock or near a tree surrounded by a soft light. That is not the picture the scriptures paint. This was a sacrifice in every sense of the word including pain, blood, and intense suffering. But as important as the Atonement is to all mankind, the biblical accounts of the event are relatively brief (Matthew 26:36–46; Mark 14:32–42; Luke 22:40–46; John 18:1). From them we know the following:

He went to the Garden of Gethsemane "as he was wont," meaning as he was accustomed to (Luke 22:39). It was a place of solitude he often enjoyed visiting. En route, the disciples began to be "sore amazed, and to be very heavy, and to complain in their hearts, wondering if this be the Messiah" (JST Mark 14:36).

Knowing their hearts, Jesus left eight of the eleven apostles near the entrance to the garden, saying, "Pray that ye enter not into temptation" (Luke 22:40). Who would tempt them? Elder James E. Talmage suggested that Satan himself was in the garden that night when the battle for the souls of all mankind was fought.[5] He tried to destroy Christ while he was praying, just as he later tried to destroy Joseph Smith while Joseph was praying (Joseph Smith–History 1:15; D&C 19:16–19). The hellish fury unleashed against Christ in Gethsemane was the most intense display of evil and darkness ever loosed on earth.

Christ took Peter, James, and John with him farther into the garden. He rebuked their doubting him and asked them to stay and watch (JST Mark 14:33–34). He returned three times, each time finding them asleep, "for they were filled with sorrow" (JST Luke 22:45).

Christ's soul was "exceeding sorrowful, even unto death" (JST Mark 14:33). Had he been mortal and not a God, he would have been crushed by the immense depression and pain. His suffering was so great that he "fell on his face" "on the ground" (Matthew 26:39; Mark 14:35).

As he prayed to God for help, he used the most intimate form of the word for "Father," *Abba*. Later, on the cross, he used a similar word of intimacy, *El*, rather than the formal *Elohim*.

Why didn't God take the pain away? The apostle John, who was there in the garden, recorded the Savior's words: "For God so loved the world, that he gave his only begotten Son, that whosoever believeth in him should not perish, but have everlasting life. For God sent not his Son into the world to condemn the world; but that the world through him might be saved" (John 3:16–17).

The Savior pleaded with the Father, "If it be possible, let this cup pass from me" (Matthew 26:39). He wanted the awful cup removed (Luke 22:42) but quickly added, "Nevertheless not my will, but thine, be done" (Luke 22:42).

An angel appeared from heaven to strengthen him (Luke 22:43). Elder Bruce R. McConkie suggested that no one other than Adam could have been that angel. Who else could have offered the strength and encouragement necessary to overcome the Fall?[6]

As the agony intensified, "he prayed more earnestly" (Luke 22:44). Some trials require more earnest prayer than others, and this was the greatest trial of all.

He suffered "more than [any person] can suffer, except it be unto death" (Mosiah 3:7). Spiritual anguish and physical pain pressed down upon him so greatly that blood oozed from every pore in his body (JST Luke 22:44; Mosiah 3:7; D&C 19:18). The medical term for such a condition is *hematodrosis*. Under extreme distress and pressure the capillaries burst and produce a bloody sweat. Christ's was the most severe instance of hematodrosis ever experienced. President Joseph Fielding Smith noted: "A great many people have an idea that when he was on the cross, and nails were driven into his hands and feet, that was his great suffering. His great suffering was before he ever was placed on the cross. It was in the Garden of Gethsemane that the blood oozed from the pores of his body: 'Which suffering caused myself, even God, the greatest of all, to tremble because of pain, and to bleed at every pore, and to suffer both body and spirit.'"[7]

Because he bled at every pore his attire must have been stained crimson when he left the Garden of Gethsemane. "No wonder, when Christ comes in power and glory, that He will come in reminding red attire (D&C 133:48), signifying not only the winepress of wrath, but also to bring to our remembrance how He suffered for each of us in Gethsemane and on Calvary!"[8]

He finally said to the Father in prayer, "If this cup may not pass away from me, except I drink it, thy will be done" (Matthew 26:42).

He suffered "pains and afflictions and temptations of every kind" (Alma 7:11), for he took upon himself *every* pain, sickness, death, infirmity, and sin of all mankind (Isaiah 53:4–5; Matthew 8:17). Elder Neal A. Maxwell observed: "The agonies of the Atonement were infinite and first-hand! Since not all human sorrow and pain is connected to sin, the full intensiveness of the Atonement involved bearing our pains, infirmities, and sicknesses, as well as our sins."[9]

There is no loneliness, grief, pain, or sin the Savior does not fully comprehend. He felt the pain of all these that he might know how to help those who suffer or who are tempted (Alma 7:12; Hebrews 2:17). His suffering filled him with mercy and empathy, and he knows how to compassionately succor us in the challenges we face. We can cast our cares upon the Lord because he is already familiar with them (1 Peter 5:7). Because he has carried our burdens, our hearts do not need to carry them any more.

His atonement covers the transgression of Adam and Eve (Mosiah 3:11; Moses 6:53); the sins and pains of the human family (Alma 7:11–13); the transgressions of those who sin in ignorance, including the mentally handicapped (Mosiah 3:11); the deaths of all little children (Mosiah 3:16, 18; D&C 137:10); and redeems from the Fall every one of the Father's creations (D&C 76:40–43).

The atonement was so important that in the Garden of Gethsemane the Savior exclaimed, "For this cause came I unto this hour" (John 12:27). He prayed that he might not "shrink." He did not want to get partway through the Atonement and then pull back, leaving something undone (D&C 19:18). He submitted himself until full payment was made. The suffering he endured equaled the combined suffering of all mankind. Why was he willing to suffer and see this through? Because he promised he would do this in the premortal life—his word was his bond. He was dependable. His example teaches us a lot about commitment. But there is another, even greater reason why he stayed: he loved us. Jesus "so loved the world that he gave his own life, that as many as would believe might become the sons of God" (D&C 34:3). His spiritual submissiveness to the Father's will saved us all. It is a marvel that he had such self-control. "I thank Him," Elder Maxwell has written, "in every situation, for maintaining His grip on Himself, which was also mankind's hold on the eternal future."[10]

When he returned the third time and found the apostles asleep, he let them sleep (JST Mark 14:42). He wakened them later as Judas arrived to betray him into the hands of the guards.

THE ATONEMENT, AN EXPRESSION OF LOVE

The Atonement is the ultimate expression of Christ's love for us. Mercifully for us, he saw it through to the end. "By means of [his atonement], if we repent, we can achieve the needed reconciliation and [eternal] emancipation."[11]

He knows perfectly and painfully well what each one of us is going through; even better than that, he knows how to help. "For we have not an high priest which cannot be touched with the feeling of our infirmities; but was in all points tempted like as we are, yet without sin. Let us therefore come boldly unto the throne of grace, that we may obtain mercy, and find grace to help in time of need" (Hebrews 4:15–16). The word *mercy* is used here to translate the Hebrew *hesed* (Hosea 6:6), which describes the love a mother feels for a child she has given birth to.

He took upon him our infirmities that his bowels might be filled with mercy. "For in that he himself hath suffered being tempted, he is able to succour them that are tempted" (Hebrews 2:18). He knows how to sympathize with us in a highly personal way. His understanding of precisely how to help us could have come in no other way. He completely comprehends our personal circumstances, including all the trials we individually face—every heartache, sorrow, illness, and challenge. His empathy "is not merely a matter of detached intellectual familiarity. He helps us, hand over hand, because He understands personally that through which we pass. No wonder we should acknowledge His hand."[12]

Thus, he can help heal any pain. He came to atone for us and can heal the brokenhearted and set at liberty those who are bruised (Luke 4:18). To Alma's people who were suffering in bondage, he said, "And I will also ease the burdens which are put upon your shoulders, that even you cannot feel them upon your backs, even while you are in bondage; and this will I do that ye may stand as witnesses for me hereafter, and that ye may know of a surety that I, the Lord God, do visit my people in their afflictions" (Mosiah 24:14).

Another marvelous thing about Christ's atonement is that even though we are far from perfect and feel so undeserving, we can "apply the atoning blood of Christ" to our lives (Mosiah 4:2) and receive his merciful help and loving kindness now, today. We can experience the blessings of the Atonement in a timely way as well as in rich abundance: "It shall be given unto you; good measure, pressed down, and shaken together, and running over" (Luke 6:38).

HIS GOOD NATURE

The Savior's endurance through his atonement also teaches another lesson. He partook of history's bitterest cup without becoming bitter. It seems so ironic that the only sinless child of God should suffer as if he had all sin. As explained above, his immense suffering enriched his empathy for us. But Christ's suffering also taught us how to pass through trials in ways that sanctify us. Those who suffer the same trials as others often have the most compassion. The Savior did not merely submit to the suffering thrust upon him, he did so in a way that enabled him to learn and grow from the experience. It is needful that we be tested and tried, "even as Abraham" (D&C 101:4). Our tests of faith and the vicissitudes of life are experiences designed for our everlasting good, if we allow them to tutor us (D&C 122:7).

The trials of mortal life help us all experience bitter and sweet contrasts in relationships with others, in love, and with our own children. Elder Maxwell observed that "in life, the sandpaper of circumstances often smooths our crustiness and patiently polishes our rough edges. There is nothing pleasant about it, however."[13] Only if we are meek, as Jesus was, can we grow from such experiences. Chastening is not pleasant. Growth is never comfortable. But if we "endure it well" we can become greater individuals and enjoy what the scriptures call the peaceable fruit of righteousness: "Now no chastening for the present seemeth to be joyous, but grievous; nevertheless, afterward it yieldeth the peaceable fruit of righteousness unto them which are exercised thereby" (JST Hebrews 12:11).

Given all that our misdeeds caused him to suffer, it is a marvelous testament of his love and mercy that the Savior does not harbor bitter feelings towards us when we commit sin. President John Taylor reminded us: "We have our weaknesses, our infirmities, follies, and foibles. It is the intention of the gospel to deliver us from these. . . . If we make any little stumbles the Savior acts not as a foolish, vindictive man, to knock another man down. He is full of kindness, long suffering, and forbearance, and treats everybody with kindness and courtesy. These are the feelings we wish to indulge in and be governed by."[14]

Because the Savior "descended below all things" (D&C 88:6), he now has power over all things. Although Jesus never committed sin, he overcame all sin. In Gethsemane, he was subjected to more pain, temptation, and sorrow than any other mortal has ever experienced, and he rose above it all. He knows how bad things are in our world, but he calmly reassures us: "In me ye might have peace. In the world ye shall have tribulation: but be of good cheer; I have overcome the world" (John 16:33).

C. S. Lewis explained: "No man knows how bad he is till he has tried very hard to be good. A silly idea is current that good people do not know what temptation means. This is an obvious lie. . . . After all, you find out the strength of [an] army by fighting against it, not by giving in. You find out the strength of a wind by trying to walk against it, not by lying down. A man who gives in to temptation after five minutes simply does not know what it would have been like an hour later. That is why bad people, in one sense, know very little about badness. They have lived a sheltered life by always giving in. We never find out the strength of the evil impulse inside us until we try to fight it; and Christ, because He was the only man who never yielded to temptation, is also the only man who knows to the full what temptation means—the only complete realist."[15]

VISIONS OF GETHSEMANE

Modern prophets have been privileged to view the scenes that took place in Gethsemane that night. Their testimonies of the Savior's sacrifice for us are sure. President Harold B. Lee, for example, bore this witness:

"As one of the humblest among you, and occupying the station I do, I want to bear you my humble testimony that I have received by the voice and the power of revelation, the knowledge and understanding that God is.

" . . . I was preparing myself for a radio talk on the Life of the Savior, when I read again the story of the life, the crucifixion and the resurrection of the Master, there came to me as I read that, a reality of that story. More than just what was on the written page. For in truth, I found myself viewing the scenes with a certainty as though I had been there in person. I know that these things come by the revelations of the living God."[16]

The final testimony shared by Elder Bruce R. McConkie just days before his death is also a powerful witness of the surety of Christ's atonement: "I am one of his witnesses, and in a coming day I shall feel the nail marks in his hands and in his feet and shall wet his feet with my tears. But I shall not know any better then than I know now that he is God's Almighty Son, that He is our Savior and Redeemer, and that salvation comes in and through His atoning blood and in no other way."[17]

NOTES

1. LDS Bible Dictionary, s.v. "balm," 618.
2. "Jesus is spoken of as the Christ and the Messiah, which means he is the one anointed of the Father to be his personal representative in all things pertaining to the salvation of mankind. The English word *Christ* is from a Greek word meaning *anointed,* and is the equivalent of *Messiah,* which is from a Hebrew and Aramaic term meaning *anointed*" (LDS Bible Dictionary, s.v. "Anointed One," 609).
3. Hafen and Hafen, "'Eve Heard All These Things and Was Glad,'" 29.
4. Maxwell, "'Willing to Submit,'" 70.
5. Talmage, *Jesus the Christ,* 613.
6. McConkie, *Mortal Messiah,* 4:124–25.
7. Smith, *Doctrines of Salvation,* 1:130.
8. Maxwell, Conference Report, April 1987, 90.
9. Maxwell, *Not My Will, But Thine,* 51.
10. Maxwell, *Even As I Am,* 115.
11. Maxwell, *One More Strain of Praise,* 91.
12. Ibid., 38.
13. Maxwell, *Notwithstanding My Weakness,* 67–68.
14. Taylor, *Journal of Discourses,* 12:81, cited in Maxwell, *Lord, Increase Our Faith,* 28.
15. Lewis, *Mere Christianity,* 124–25.
16. Lee, *Divine Revelation,* 10.
17. McConkie, *New Witness,* xvi.

BETRAYAL AND TRIALS 6

He was taken from prison and from judgment.
—Isaiah 53:8

The ministry of the Messiah was filled with irony. At no time were the tragic ironies leading to his death more pronounced than on the night of his betrayal. Dr. Robert L. Millet summarized how grim those ironies were: "During the hours of atonement, for example, he who had remained sinless became, as it were, the great sinner. In the language of Paul, God the Father 'made him to be sin for us, who knew no sin' (2 Corinthians 5:21). To the Galatian Saints, Paul taught that 'Christ hath redeemed us from the curse of the law, being made a curse for us' (Galatians 3:13). He who deserved least of all to suffer suffered the most—more than mortal mind can fathom. He who had brought life—the more abundant life (see John 10:10)—subjected himself to the powers of death and darkness.

"Notwithstanding all the sufferings and the infinite opposition faced by the Infinite One, the Prophet testified that the Savior 'kept the law of God and remained without sin, showing thereby that it is in the power of man to keep the law and remain also without sin. And also that by him a righteous judgment might come upon all flesh, that all who walk not in the law of God may justly be condemned by the law and have no excuse for their sins' ([*Lectures on Faith*] 5:2). Jesus never took a backward step or a moral detour. He 'was in all points tempted like as we are, yet without sin' (Hebrews 4:15; see also 1 Peter 2:22)."[1]

Christ came to save us, yet he refused to save himself. He taught us to endure to the end and submit to the will of the Father, and he was the perfect example of one who suffered unjustly at the hands of wicked men for humbly submitting to do the will of the Father. He did so without complaint. He was poised and filled with dignity. He was the consummate gentleman.[2] Everything he taught us about handling injustice, he personally demonstrated, from turning the other cheek, to praying for those who despitefully use us, to showing love to enemies. He is a perfect example, and on the eve of his final sacrifice, he demonstrated profound meekness and depth of character.

JUDAS' BETRAYAL

After Judas left the Upper Room (map, page xii, location 7), he went to the seat of the chief priests and Pharisees (8). They too were observing the Passover. The ironies are too great to be ignored. They were eating a firstborn male lamb without blemish. From the way they would treat the Lamb of God that night, we can only guess how little the symbols of the Passover really meant to them.

Judas "received a band of men and officers from the chief priests and Pharisees" (John 18:3) and then went back to the Upper Room. By the time he arrived, the Savior and the apostles had already gone to Gethsemane. It may have taken Judas several hours to figure out where they were. They eventually came to the garden "with lanterns and torches and weapons" (John 18:3). This was an armed mob of no small size. A band of soldiers was enough to put down an uprising (Matthew 27:27).

As they approached, Judas "gave them a sign, saying, Whomsoever I shall kiss, that same is he: hold him fast. And forthwith he came to Jesus, and said, Hail, master; and kissed him" (Matthew 26:48–49). Jesus "said unto him, Friend, wherefore art thou come?" (Matthew 26:50). The Savior taught us, "Love your enemies, bless them that curse you, do good to them that hate you" (Matthew 5:44), and he showed us the way. The ability to look beyond an individual's shortcomings and still show love and warmth to him or her is a trait of godliness.

Sometimes in our dealings with one another we may be tempted to render quick judgments about another person's character and then treat that person accordingly. There are two kinds of judging: "final judgments, which we are forbidden to make, and intermediate judgments which we are directed to make, but upon righteous principles," Elder Dallin H. Oaks taught. Final judgment belongs to the Lord. But righteous intermediate judgments need to be made daily. Intermediate judgments "refrain from judging people and only judge situations. . . . [They] refrain from declaring that a person has forfeited all opportunity for exaltation or even all opportunity for a useful role in the work of the Lord. The gospel is a gospel of hope, and none of us is authorized to deny the power of the Atonement to bring about a cleansing of individual sins, forgiveness, and a reformation of life on appropriate conditions."[3]

Even the Savior in his dealings with Judas refrained from making a final judgment. He called him "friend" at the moment Judas was betraying Him. He gave Judas every opportunity to turn back, but Judas foolishly refused. No doubt Judas will feel that same intensity of love and concern from God at the final day of judgment, when he is commanded to depart from His presence because of his deeds.

Judas' refusal to receive Christ's love also added to the Savior's suffering. As Edith Hamilton astutely observed, "When love meets no return, the result is suffering, and the greater the love the greater the suffering. There can be no greater suffering than to love purely and perfectly one who is bent on evil and self-destruction. That was what God endured at the hands of men."[4] God loves us that much, and there are times when we come to know and understand that kind of love ourselves. Elder Neal A. Maxwell commented: "Many parents and some spouses love and care but experience unreciprocated love. This is part of coming to know, on our small scale, what Jesus experienced."[5]

THE ARREST

The Savior, "knowing all things that should come upon him, went forth, and said unto them [the band of soldiers], Whom seek ye? They answered him, Jesus of Nazareth. Jesus saith unto them, I am he. . . . As soon then as he had said unto them, I am he, they went backward, and fell to the ground" (John 18:4–6).

Why would they fall down? What knocked them over and sent them tumbling "to the ground"? Obviously the Savior was sending a very clear message. He was Jehovah, the God of creation and the Redeemer of Israel. The words he spoke, "I am,"[6] were the very same words the premortal Jesus (Jehovah) told Moses to deliver to the children of Israel when Moses asked whom he should say sent him to deliver them. "And God said unto Moses, I AM THAT I AM: . . . Thus shalt thou say unto the children of Israel, I AM hath sent me unto you" (Exodus 3:14). "I AM" means in Hebrew "YAHVEH," or Jehovah. When Christ announced to the soldiers "I am," he was telling them he was Jehovah. It may have been the Spirit accompanying his declaration that caused all of them to fall to the ground. A similar thing happened to Abinadi, when he stood before wicked King Noah and his priests (Mosiah 13:2–3), and to Nephi, when his brothers attempted to lay hands upon him: "Whoso shall lay his hands upon me . . . shall be as naught before the power of God, for God shall smite him" (1 Nephi 17:47–48). It was as if the Savior were saying to the soldiers, "I lay down my life, that I might take it again. No man taketh it from me, but I lay it down of myself" (JST John 10:17–18). No armed mob, no band of soldiers could take his life. It was a freewill offering, offered only when he willed it.

As the guards stood back up and stepped forward to take him, Peter tried to stop the arrest. He drew his sword (or long knife, in Hebrew) and struck at the high priest's servant, Malchus. Peter missed striking him down, but the blow cut off the man's right ear (JST John 18:10).

Given his own agony, it would have been easy for the Savior to overlook his assailant's painful loss. But the ever-merciful "Jesus . . . touched his ear and healed him" (JST Luke 22:51).

"Then said Jesus unto Peter, Put up thy sword into the sheath: the cup which my Father hath given me, shall I not drink it?" (John 18:11). He added, "Thinkest thou that I cannot now pray to my Father, and he shall presently give me more than twelve legions of angels? But how then shall the scriptures be fulfilled, that thus it must be?" (Matthew 26:53–54).

When his disciples heard this saying, they "all forsook him and fled" (JST Mark 14:56). Anyone associated with him was in danger, including innocent bystanders: "And there followed him a certain young man, a disciple, having a linen cloth cast about his naked body; and the young man laid hold on him, and he left the linen cloth and fled from them naked, and saved himself out of their hands" (JST Mark 14:57).

The Savior addressed his captors and said to the chief priests, captains of the temple, and the elders, who had come to him: "Are ye come out as against a thief, with swords and staves? When I was daily with you in the temple, ye stretched forth no hands against me; but this is your hour, and the power of darkness" (JST Luke 22:52–53).

Then "took they him, and led him, and brought him into the high priest's house" (JST Luke 22:54; see map, page xii, location 8.) John the Beloved followed closely behind (John 18:15), and "Peter followed "afar off" (JST Luke 22:54).

TAKEN TO THE PALACE OF ANNAS AND CAIAPHAS

Annas had been appointed high priest in A.D. 7 by the Roman legate Quirinius but was removed in A.D. 15 by Valerius Gratus. His son-in-law Joseph Caiaphas was high priest at the time of Jesus' arrest. "During this time Annas was a person of great influence in the Sanhedrin. Jesus . . . was first brought to him. . . . In accordance with Jewish custom he kept the title 'high priest' after he was deposed from office."[7]

The interview with Annas was brief: "The high priest then asked Jesus of his disciples, and of his doctrine.

"Jesus answered him, I spake openly to the world; I ever taught in the synagogue, and in the temple, whither the Jews always resort; and in secret have I said nothing.

"Why askest thou me? ask them which heard me, what I have said unto them: behold, they know what I said.

"And when he had thus spoken, one of the officers which stood by struck Jesus with the palm of his hand, saying, Answerest thou the high priest so?

"Jesus answered him, If I have spoken evil, bear witness of the evil: but if well, why smitest thou me?

"Now Annas had sent him bound unto Caiaphas the high priest" (John 18:19–24).

TRIED BEFORE CAIAPHAS AND THE SANHEDRIN

As the officiating high priest, Caiaphas was responsible to offer the intercessory prayer in behalf of all Israel to begin the Passover sacrifices and the Passover meal. Ironically, Caiaphas had been inspired to counsel the Jews that "it was expedient that one man should die for the people," foreshadowing the Savior's sacrifice (John 18:14). He must not have realized the role he and his council were about to play in fulfilling his own prophecy.

Filled with darkness and evil desires, the members of the Sanhedrin had long desired an opportunity to destroy Jesus. Caiaphas and all the council members sought for false witnesses against Jesus so they could have him put to death. But "though many false witnesses came, they found none that could accuse him" (JST Matthew 26:59). So Jesus was charged with sedition (being a disturber of the peace) because, the witnesses said, he claimed to be able to destroy the temple of God and build it again in three days. But their recollections of exactly what he said conflicted. Jesus held his peace and stood in majestic silence while they argued and falsely accused him. Filled with anger, Caiaphas cried out: "Answerest thou nothing? Knowest thou what these witness against thee? . . . I adjure thee by the living God, that thou tell us whether thou be the Christ, the Son of God" (JST Matthew 26:61–64).

The Savior answered: "I am" (Mark 14:62).

Then Caiaphas "rent his clothes" and said, "What further need have we of witnesses? Behold, now, ye have heard his blasphemy.

What think ye? They answered and said, He is guilty, and worthy of death" (JST Matthew 26:66–67).

Blasphemy, which is falsely claiming the power of God, was the most serious charge in Jewish law. "One of the greatest ironies in history occurred, for Jesus, the divine Son of God, the one person who could not have been guilty of *falsely* assuming the power of God, was found guilty of blasphemy! . . . The only person since the fall of Adam who had power over physical death was condemned to die!"[8]

The Joseph Smith Translation records that the entire council condemned him (JST Mark 15:1–2). It is clear from the Joseph Smith Translation that personal transgression was at the heart of the betrayal. "Other translations [of the Bible]," Dr. Thomas E. Sherry has noted, "link much of the rejection to cultural reasons but in the Joseph Smith Translation it is linked primarily to personal sin. . . . Wickedness diminishes faith, belief, and spiritual sensitivity."[9]

During his ministry among them, the Savior consistently called these people to repentance for their hypocrisy with such strong statements as the following:

"Ye know not Moses, neither the prophets; for if ye had known them, ye would have believed on me; for to this intent they were written" (JST Luke 14:36).

"Except ye repent, the preaching of John shall condemn you in the day of judgment. . . . I speak in parables; that your unrighteousness may be rewarded unto you" (JST Matthew 21:34).

"Ye have kept not the ordinances of God; . . . ye keep not the law" (JST Mark 7:12).

"And Jesus said unto his disciples, Beholdest thou the Scribes, and the Pharisees, and the Priests, and the Levites? They teach in their synagogues, but do not observe the law, nor the commandments; and all have gone out of the way, and are under sin.

"Go thou and say unto them, Why teach ye men the law and the commandments, when ye yourselves are the children of corruption?

"Say unto them, Ye hypocrites, first cast out the beam out of thine own eye; and then shalt thou see clearly to cast out the mote out of thy brother's eye" (JST Matthew 7:6–8).

"Ye blind guides, who strain at a gnat, and swallow a camel; who make yourselves appear unto men that ye would not commit the least sin, and yet ye yourselves, transgress the whole law.

"Woe unto you, Scribes and Pharisees, hypocrites! For ye make clean the outside of the cup, and of the platter; but within they are full of extortion and excess.

"Ye blind Pharisees! Cleanse first the cup and platter within, that the outside of them may be clean also.

"Woe unto you, Scribes and Pharisees, hypocrites! For ye are like unto whited sepulchres, which indeed appear beautiful outwardly, but are within full of the bones of the dead, and of all uncleanness.

"Even so, ye also outwardly appear righteous unto men, but within ye are full of hypocrisy and iniquity" (JST Matthew 23:21–25).

"Woe unto you, lawyers! For ye have taken away the key of knowledge, the fulness of the scriptures; ye enter not in yourselves into the kingdom; and those who were entering in, ye hindered" (JST Luke 11:53).

"And why teach ye the law, and deny that which is written; and condemn him whom the Father hath sent to fulfill the law, that ye might all be redeemed?

"O fools! for you have said in your hearts, There is no God. And you pervert the right way; and the kingdom of heaven suffereth violence of you; and you persecute the meek; and in your violence you seek to destroy the kingdom; and ye take the children of the kingdom by force. Woe unto you, ye adulterers!

"And they reviled him again, being angry for the saying, that they were adulterers" (JST Luke 16:20–22).

Enraged for some time against him, the chief priests of the Sanhedrin now unleashed their fury on him. They mocked him, smote him, and spat in his face (Matthew 26:67). They blindfolded him and then struck him on the face and taunted him, "Prophesy, who is it who smote thee? And many other things blasphemously spake they against him" (JST Luke 22:64–65). It was ironic for them to accuse him of blasphemy and then blaspheme against him themselves. Their hypocrisy "doth witness against them . . . for they have rewarded evil unto themselves!" (2 Nephi 13:9). President Ezra Taft

Benson said, "It was through pride that Christ was crucified. The Pharisees were wroth because Jesus claimed to be the Son of God, which was a threat to their position, and so they plotted His death. (See John 11:53)."[10]

Their vile mockings and illicit trial lasted the entire night. It was morning when the chief priests consulted with the elders and scribes how to put Jesus to death (Matthew 27:1). They decided to interrogate him one last time:

"Art thou the Christ? Tell us. And he said unto them, If I tell you, ye will not believe.

"And if I also ask you, ye will not answer me, nor let me go.

"Hereafter shall the Son of Man sit on the right hand of the power of God.

"Then said they all, Art thou then the Son of God? And he said unto them, Ye say that I am.

"And they said, What need we of any further witness? For we ourselves have heard of his own mouth" (JST Luke 22:67–71).

"And the whole council condemned him" (JST Mark 15:2).

PETER'S DENIAL

Peter was standing nearby in the open-air hallway just outside the council chamber. He was standing beside a fire pit, "for it was cold: and they warmed themselves" (John 18:18).

A young damsel nearby "earnestly looked upon him, and said, This man was also with him." "Art not thou also one of this man's disciples?" (Luke 22:56; John 18:17). Peter replied, "I am not." "Woman, I know him not" (John 18:17; Luke 22:57).

Peter left and went out on the porch. Another maiden said, "This is one of them" (Mark 14:69). Peter denied it again and said, "I am not" (John 18:25).

A third time he was accosted, "Surely thou also art one of them; for thy speech bewrayeth thee. Then began he to curse and to swear, saying, I know not the man. And immediately the cock crew" (Matthew 26:73–74).

"And the Lord turned, and looked upon Peter" (Luke 22:61).

"And Peter called to mind the words which Jesus said unto him, Before the cock crow twice, thou shalt deny me thrice. And he went out, and fell upon his face, and wept bitterly" (JST Mark 14:81–82).

Later, at the Sea of Galilee, the resurrected Savior appeared to Peter and asked him three times, "Lovest thou me?" (John 21:15–17).

JUDAS COMMITS SUICIDE

"Then Judas, who had betrayed him, when he saw that he was condemned, repented himself, and brought again the thirty pieces of silver to the chief priests and elders,

"Saying, I have sinned in that I have betrayed the innocent blood.

"And they said unto him, What is that to us? See thou to it; thy sins be upon thee.

"And he cast down the pieces of silver in the temple, and departed, and went, and hanged himself on a tree. And straightway he fell down, and his bowels gushed out, and he died.

"And the chief priests took the silver pieces, and said, It is not lawful for to put them in the treasury, because it is the price of blood.

"And they took counsel, and bought with them the potter's field, to bury strangers in. Wherefore that field was called, The field of blood, unto this day.

"Then was fulfilled that which was spoken by Jeremy [Jeremiah], the prophet, saying, And they took the thirty pieces of silver, the price of him that was valued, whom they of the children of Israel did value.

"And therefore they took the pieces of silver, and gave them for the potter's field, as the Lord appointed by the mouth of Jeremy [Jeremiah]" (JST Matthew 27:3–10).

TRIED BEFORE PILATE

The power to carry out capital punishment had been taken away from the Sanhedrin by the Romans (John 18:31). The council had to deliver Jesus to Pontius Pilate for an official decree of death to be issued. The council and "the whole multitude of them" (Luke 23:1) led Christ from Caiaphas' Palace (map, page xii, location 8) to Antonia Fortress (9).

Pilate lived in Caesarea but was visiting Jerusalem during Passover and staying in Antonia Fortress. One of the exits from Antonia Fortress spilled down a large staircase into the temple courtyard so that soldiers could quickly disperse any gatherings or uprisings. A large crowd of people had gathered in the courtyard when Pilate took Jesus inside the fortress to hear the matter.

The charge against Jesus was changed by the Sanhedrin from blasphemy against God to high treason against Rome: "We found this man perverting the nation, and forbidding to give tribute to Caesar, saying that he himself is Christ, a king" (JST Luke 23:2). Ironically, Christ's words were "render . . . unto Caesar the things which are Caesar's" (Matthew 22:21).

Pilate asked Jesus, "Art thou the King of the Jews?

"Jesus answered him, Sayest thou this thing of thyself, or did others tell it thee of me?

"Pilate answered, Am I a Jew? Thine own nation and the chief priests have delivered thee unto me; what hast thou done?

"Jesus answered, My kingdom is not of this world; if my kingdom were of this world, then would my servants fight, that I should not be delivered to the Jews; but now is my kingdom not from hence.

"Pilate therefore said unto him, Art thou a king then? Jesus answered, Thou sayest that I am a king. To this end was I born, and for this cause came I into the world, that I should bear witness unto the truth. Every one that is of the truth heareth my voice.

"Pilate saith unto him, What is truth? And when he had said this, he went out again unto the Jews, and saith unto them, I find in him no fault" (JST John 18:33–38).

Pilate was about to set the Savior free. The chief priests "were the more fierce" in stirring up the crowd to anger (Luke 23:5). One of them cried out that Jesus had been teaching treason "beginning from Galilee to this place" (Luke 23:5).

Upon learning that Jesus was from Galilee, Pilate decided to send him to Herod to be tried. Herod was the ruler of Galilee, and he was visiting Jerusalem at the time of the Passover. The angry multitude proceeded from Antonia Fortress (map, page xii, location 9) to Herod's palace (10).

BEFORE HEROD

"When Herod saw Jesus, he was exceeding glad: for he was desirous to see him of a long season, because he had heard many things of him; and he hoped to have seen some miracle done by him" (Luke 23:8). Earlier in his ministry the Savior had warned about those who seek miracles. His teaching gives us great insight into Herod's flawed character: "A wicked and adulterous generation seeketh after a sign" (Matthew 16:4).

Herod "questioned with him in many words," but the Savior "answered him nothing." The chief priests and scribes "vehemently accused him," but Christ stood there quietly (Luke 23:9–10). Isaiah had foreseen this event: "He was oppressed, and he was afflicted, yet he opened not his mouth: he is brought as a lamb to the slaughter, and as a sheep before her shearers is dumb, so he openeth not his mouth" (Isaiah 53:7).

Angered by his silence, Herod and his soldiers mocked the Savior. They arrayed him in a "gorgeous robe" (JST Luke 23:11) to ridicule him and then sent him again to Pilate at Antonia Fortress. Luke records an interesting moment: "And the same day Pilate and Herod were made friends together; for before this they were at enmity between themselves" (JST Luke 23:12).

Elder Neal A. Maxwell offered a marvelous insight into the Savior's character that emerges from this unholy alliance: "Being meek and lowly in character, majestic Jesus was uninterested in power per se. He repeatedly refused to use his power inappropriately even to lessen his awful suffering during his temptations and atonement. . . . For example, previous to Gethsemane and the Crucifixion Pilate and Herod had been 'at enmity,' yet in response to the crisis which Jesus' presence created, they 'made friends together' (Luke 23:12). Opportunities doubtless existed for Jesus to take advantage of their temporary alliance in order to please them. Thereby he might have reduced at least some of his suffering if he had been willing to shrink, even partially, from going through with all of the full agonies of the Atonement (see D&C 19:18, 19).

"After all, Pilate found no fault with Jesus. Herod, too, was probably reachable, having been desirous 'to see [Jesus] of a long season,' hoping 'to have seen some miracle done by him' (Luke 23:8–9). Yet, standing before Herod, fully aware of the ruler's expectations and with a chance to please him, Jesus 'answered him nothing' (Luke 23:9; see also Mosiah 14:7). There would be no demonstration to purchase even slight amelioration. Jesus gave no consolation to inquiring Pilate either. Jesus' integrity was never for sale. There was such strength in His meekness, whereas a lesser individual would have gladly seized upon any opportunity for relief. But anointed Jesus' character was such that He would not shrink from His appointed and agonizing task."[11]

SECOND APPEARANCE BEFORE PILATE

Throughout this ordeal, the Savior's example teaches us much about endurance. Despite all that he suffered—more than thirty-six hours without sleep, extensive walking (several miles) while bound, intense agony and great loss of blood, no food, and physical abuse (he was struck, mocked, spat upon, and scourged)—Jesus never once lost control of himself or of the situation.[12] He was fully composed and in total control. Why did he suffer the humiliation and pain? He could have spoken one word and all his tormentors would have been annihilated. Why did he submit to them? Two reasons are mentioned in the scriptural record: because he wanted to do the will of his Father, and "because of his loving kindness . . . towards the children of men" (1 Nephi 19:9).

Pilate's wife warned Pilate of a dream she had had about Jesus: "When he was set down on the judgment-seat, his wife sent unto him, saying, Have thou nothing to do with that just man, for I have suffered many things this day in a vision because of him" (JST Matthew 27:20).

Members of the Sanhedrin, however, were determined to put Jesus to death. Pilate called the chief priests, the rulers, and the people together and said, "You have brought this man unto me, as one who perverteth the people; and behold, I, having examined him before you, have found no fault in this man, touching those things whereof ye accuse him. No, nor yet Herod; for I sent you to him; and lo, nothing worthy of death is done unto him; I will therefore chastise him, and release him" (JST Luke 23:14–16).

Even Pilate's offer to have him chastised, meaning beaten with a whip, did not appease the bloodthirsty mob. So Pilate pointed out that it was common for him to release one prisoner at Passover and made an offer: "Whom will ye that I release unto you? Barabbas [a murderer], or Jesus which is called Christ?" (Matthew 27:17).

The chief priests "moved the people" and "persuaded the multitude" to ask for Barabbas and destroy Jesus (Mark 15:11; Matthew 27:20). The people cried out all at once "Barabbas" (Luke 23:18).

It is ironic that Barabbas (whose name in Aramaic means "son of the father") was released from prison, but the true Son of the Father was condemned to death. Even this event bore witness of Christ's atoning sacrifice: a sinful son of the Father was freed from death when the true Son of God was condemned. Similarly, we have broken the laws of God and are consigned to spiritual death, but the death of the Firstborn of the Father sets us free from the grasp of "this awful monster . . . , death and hell" (2 Nephi 9:10).

All the people began to cry, "Deliver him unto us to be crucified. Away with him" (JST Mark 15:15). They chanted, "Crucify him, crucify him" (Luke 23:21).

HE IS SCOURGED AND MOCKED

Pilate said, "Why, what evil hath he done? I have found no cause of death in him: I will therefore chastise him, and let him go" (Luke 23:22).

"Then the soldiers of the governor took Jesus into the common hall, and gathered unto him the whole band.

"And they stripped him, and put on him a purple robe.

"And when they had platted a crown of thorns, they put it upon his head, and a reed in his right hand; and they bowed the knee before him, and they mocked him, saying, Hail, King of the Jews!

"And they spit upon him, and took the reed, and smote him on the head" (JST Matthew 27:29–32).

This mocking by the soldiers was done in the form of a cruel game called the game of kings. A game piece was rolled, and whatever kingly description it fell on would then be acted out against the prisoner in a mocking way. (A game board for the game of kings may still be seen in Jerusalem in the Church of Flagellation and the Sisters of Zion.)

The true King of the Jews was crowned and arrayed in a robe reserved for royalty (Matthew 27:28–29; Luke 23:11; John 19:2). The color of the robe was purple, the color of royalty (JST Matthew 27:30). His coat, or robe, was seamless, as the high priest's robe was required to be (John 19:23–24; Exodus 28:31–32). He was King and High Priest and Sacrificial Lamb. Ironically, the Jews' recognition of his authority was done in derision rather than admiration.

He was scourged with a whip embedded with pieces of metal and jagged bone. The scourging alone was enough to take the life of most men. But the Savior was not yet ready to offer his life.

Pilate had him taken before the people "wearing the crown of thorns, and the purple robe," saying to the mob, "Behold the man!" (John 19:5). It is ironic that despite the spiritual confirmations that are given, some, like Pilate, consider Christ only a "man."

Still not satisfied, the crowd continued to call for crucifixion. Pilate began to fear the people.

"[He] went again into the judgment hall, and saith unto Jesus, Whence art thou? But Jesus gave him no answer.

"Then saith Pilate unto him, Speakest thou not unto me? knowest thou not that I have power to crucify thee, and have power to release thee?

"Jesus answered, Thou couldest have no power against me, except it were given thee from above; therefore he that delivered me unto thee hath the greater sin.

"And from thenceforth Pilate sought to release him; but the Jews cried out, saying, If thou let this man go, thou art not Caesar's friend; whosoever maketh himself a king speaketh against Caesar.

"When Pilate therefore heard that saying, he brought Jesus forth, and sat down in the judgment seat in a place called the Pavement, but in the Hebrew, Gabbatha.

"And it was the preparation of the passover, and about the sixth hour; and he saith unto the Jews, Behold your King!" (JST John 19:9–14).

The people immediately cried out "more exceedingly, Crucify him"; "Let him be crucified" (Mark 15:14; Matthew 27:23).

"When Pilate saw that he could prevail nothing, but rather that a tumult was made, he took water, and washed his hands before the multitude, saying, I am innocent of the blood of this just person; see that ye do nothing unto him.

"Then answered all the people, and said, His blood come upon us and our children" (JST Matthew 27:26–27).

The weak and vacillating Roman governor gave in to their demands and swept aside his own orders. He released Barabbas and delivered Jesus "to their will" to be crucified (Luke 23:25; John 19:16). Pilate delivered the Lamb of God to be crucified during the very week the paschal lambs had been slaughtered (John 19:14).

The Book of Mormon teaches that "there is none other nation on earth that would crucify their God" (2 Nephi 10:3). "For should the mighty miracles be wrought among other nations they would repent, and know that he be their God. But because of priestcrafts and iniquities, they at Jerusalem will stiffen their necks against him, that he be crucified" (2 Nephi 10:4–5). Their religious leaders "trample[d him] under their feet," set him at "naught" (treated him as being totally insignificant), and "hearken[ed] not to the voice of his counsels" (1 Nephi 19:7).

ENDURING IRONY

Injustices happen to all of us. But the events leading to the crucifixion of the Savior were filled with incredibly tragic and undeserved events. He endured more irony than we will ever experience. For example, Christ created the earth for us, placed it in an orbit that would sustain life, and gave it to us so that we might become like our Father in Heaven (1 Nephi 17:35), yet when he was born on the earth, there was no room anywhere for him (JST Luke 2:7).

He created the universe that surrounds us, including perhaps millions of planets like ours (Moses 1:27–35; D&C 88:45, 47), yet some who study the heavens deny the very existence of a divine Creator. The "Big Bang Theory," for instance, claims that the patterned and orderly universe began with a chance and random explosion rather than an intelligent and divine Creator's hand—as if an explosion in a print shop could produce an orderly, compiled dictionary!

Christ has the brightest mind and keenest intellect—the Light of Christ enlightens every mind on earth—yet there seems to be little room in the intellect of many in today's world for him and his teachings.[13]

He showed kindness and consideration to Judas, who disdainfully betrayed him with a kiss (Matthew 26:48). He is familiar with every painful emotion we experience, "including even the feeling of being forsaken."[14]

He was arrested by a band of soldiers but could have called down legions of angels to protect himself (Matthew 26:53).

He who knows all things was taunted to prophesy which one of his assailants was hitting him (JST Matthew 26:68).

Perhaps the greatest irony was the Atonement. Jesus was the only sinless child of our Father in Heaven, yet he suffered the pains of every sin. Elder Neal A. Maxwell called this the "awful arithmetic"[15] of the Atonement. When we begin to feel that life has not been much of a rose garden, we should "remember who wore the crown of thorns."[16]

The Roman governor "marvelled greatly" that Christ refused to answer the questions asked by his accusers (Matthew 27:14). When he told them who he was, they charged him with blasphemy. When he didn't answer, they were angry. They weren't really seeking answers, just laying snares and verbal traps.

A man whose name means "son of the father" was freed from death, and the true "Son of the Father" was condemned to die (Matthew 27:26).

A poem by an unknown author illustrates other ironies associated with the Savior's selflessness and mercy:

> *He who is the bread of life began his ministry hungering.*
> *He who is the water of life ended his ministry thirsting.*
> *He was weary, yet he is our rest.*
> *He paid tribute, and yet he is our King.*
> *He prayed, yet he hears prayers.*

He wept, but he dries our tears.
He was sold for thirty pieces of silver, yet he redeemed the world.
He was led as a lamb to the slaughter, but he is the Good Shepherd.
He died and gave his life and by dying destroyed death.

NOTES

1. Millet, *Selected Writings,* 228–29.
2. I am indebted to Mary Jane Woodger for bringing this description to my attention.
3. Oaks, "'Judge Not' and Judging," 6–13.
4. Hamilton, *Spokesman for God,* 112, as cited in Maxwell, "O How Great the Plan," 5.
5. Maxwell, "O How Great the Plan," 5.
6. John 18:15 in the King James Version records Jesus as saying "I am *he.*" Note that the word *he* is in italics. Italicized words were added by the King James translators to "round out and complete the sense of a phrase, but were not present in the Hebrew or Greek text of the manuscript used" (LDS Bible Dictionary, s.v. "italics," 708). So the phrase the Savior used was "I AM," not "I am *he.*"
7. LDS Bible Dictionary, s.v. "Annas," 609.
8. Ludlow, "Greatest Week in History," 42.
9. Sherry, "Christ, Savior, Son of God."
10. Benson, "Beware of Pride," 5.
11. Maxwell, *Lord, Increase Our Faith,* 24–25.
12. I am indebted to Gerald N. Lund for this insight.
13. I am indebted to Elder Neal A. Maxwell for this insight.
14. Maxwell, Conference Report, April 1987, 89.
15. Maxwell, "'Willing to Submit,'" 73.
16. Maxwell, Conference Report, April 1987, 89.

"BEHOLD, THE GREAT REDEEMER DIE"

7

Truly this was the Son of God.
—Matthew 27:54

The Savior was taken from Antonia Fortress (map, page xii, location 9) to the hill Golgotha (11). Golgotha lay just outside the city wall. The sin offering of the law of Moses was always offered "without the camp," or outside the camp of Israel (Exodus 29:14; Leviticus 4:11–12; Numbers 19:3–5). Like the sin offering of the ancient law, Jesus was crucified outside the city wall (Hebrews 13:10–13).

With the wooden cross on his back, Jesus began the walk towards the northern extremity of Mount Moriah. The Only Begotten of the Father was carrying the wood upon which he was to be sacrificed. Hundreds of years earlier Abraham had taken the wood of the burnt offering, laid it upon Isaac's back (his only begotten son of Sariah), and ascended another part of the same hill (Genesis 22:7). For Christ, however, there would be no ram in the thicket.

As he proceeded along the way, Jesus stumbled under the weight of his cross. His tired physical body was too weakened by his suffering and the abuse to carry the cross any farther. The Roman soldiers compelled Simon, a man of Cyrene, to bear the cross for him. We don't know what words may have been exchanged, if any, between Christ and Simon, but later, Simon's son became one of the disciples (Mark 15:21; Romans 16:13).

A "great company" followed the solemn procession, bewailing and lamenting. Jesus turned to them and offered words of consolation. He warned them about the persecutions Rome would later inflict on the inhabitants of Jerusalem: "Daughters of Jerusalem, weep not for me, but weep for yourselves, and for your children.

"For behold, the days are coming, in the which they shall say, Blessed are the barren, and the wombs which never bare, and the paps which never gave suck.

"Then shall they begin to say to the mountains, Fall on us; and to the hills, Cover us.

"And if these things are done in the green tree, what shall be done in the dry tree?" (JST Luke 23:27–31).

It was about the third hour (or 9:00 A.M.) when the Savior was nailed to the cross. As they began the crucifixion, the soldiers offered him vinegar mixed with gall, a crude painkiller. He refused the sedative and took every pain unanesthetized and in full force, just as he had the night before in Gethsemane.

Mallets drove nails through his palms and wrists, as Isaiah had foreseen: "And I will fasten him as a nail in a sure place" (Isaiah 22:23). The Psalmist described the event with these words, "For dogs have compassed me; the assembly of the wicked have enclosed me; they pierced my hands and my feet" (JST Psalm 22:16). His meekness and his empathy for his executioners, even while suffering intense pain at their hands, gives us something to think about. As they nailed him to the cross and then hoisted him painfully up and dropped the cross into place, all Jesus said was, "Father, forgive them; for they know not what they do. (Meaning the soldiers who crucified him)" (JST Luke 23:35).[1]

How does one do that? What depth of character does it require to forgive an enemy, let alone an enemy who is inflicting serious pain and injury? It's relatively easy to forgive someone who has asked for forgiveness, especially if time has passed. But what about those who have recently hurt us, who have not asked for forgiveness, or who are still causing the hurt? The Savior taught, "Pray for them which despitefully use you" and "love your enemies" (Matthew 5:44). The ability to "frankly forgive them all that they had done" (1 Nephi 7:21) is possible only for those filled with the same spirit of love that God has—charity, the pure love of Christ. It is the kind of love God has for all his children.

Jesus was lifted up on the cross, just as the brazen serpent of Moses' day had been lifted up (Helaman 8:14–15; John 3:14–15). Those who looked up to the brazen serpent on the cross were healed (Numbers 21:6–9). In like manner, all who look to Christ will not perish but "live, even unto that life which is eternal" (Helaman 8:15).

He was stripped of his clothing and left to hang in shame. He suffered great pain and humiliation. His executioners cast lots for his garments as prophesied: "They part my garments among them, and cast lots upon my vesture" (Psalm 22:18).

By order of Pilate a plaque was hung on the cross: "JESUS OF NAZARETH, THE KING OF THE JEWS, in letters of Greek, and Latin, and Hebrew.

"And the chief priests said unto Pilate, It should be written and set up over his head, his accusation, This is he that said he was Jesus, the King of the Jews.

"But Pilate answered and said, What I have written, I have written; let it alone" (JST Matthew 27:40–42).

Jesus was crucified between two thieves, as Isaiah had foreseen: "He made his grave with the wicked" (Isaiah 53:9).

Standing by the base of the cross were his mother, Mary, her sister, and Mary Magdalene (John 19:25). A woman's nature, typically, is to want to help and comfort others who are suffering, and not surprisingly, Mary's sister was standing beside her in her hour of grief.

STATEMENTS ON THE CROSS

After the cross was set in place, the minutes slowly turned to hours. We can only imagine the agony of being crucified. His suffering on the cross extended from about 9:00 A.M. to 6:00 P.M., approximately nine hours.

The spite and jeering of the crowds was vicious: "And they who passed by railed on him, wagging their heads, and saying, Ah, thou who destroyest the temple and buildest it in three days, save thyself, and come down from the cross" (JST Mark 15:34).

"If thou be the Son of God come down from the cross" (JST Matthew 27:44).

This was the same diabolical phrase used by Satan to tempt him at the beginning of his ministry: "If thou be the Son of God," followed by a challenge to perform some miracle (Matthew 4:3, 6). Lucifer always wants us to doubt who we are. He knows that hearts filled with doubt cannot exercise faith.

The taunts came from many groups: "Likewise also the chief priests mocking with the Scribes and elders, said, He saved others, himself he cannot save. If he be the King of Israel, let him now come down from the cross, and we will believe him.

"He trusted in God; let him deliver him now; if he will save him, let him save him; for he said, I am the Son of God" (JST Matthew 27:45–46).

"And the soldiers also mocked him, coming to him, and offering him vinegar, and saying, If thou be the King of the Jews, save thyself" (JST Luke 23:37–38).

Even this scornful mocking fulfilled prophecy. Isaiah said the bloodthirsty mob who crucified the Savior would "esteem him stricken, smitten of God" (Isaiah 53:4). They had no compassion for him, despite all the compassion he had shown them during his ministry and especially the night before in Gethsemane.

According to the law of Moses, those worthy of death were to be hanged from a tree because they were "accursed of God" (Deuteronomy 21:23; Galatians 3:13). That is why the brazen serpent was raised up on the pole by Moses. Since the time of the Garden of Eden, the serpent has been a type of Satan, "the accursed of God." The plague of fiery serpents that brought great pain and even death to the children of Israel represents the wounds inflicted on mortals by Satan. Satan has power to bruise us and sting us with "fiery darts" of temptation (1 Nephi 15:24), but he will eventually be crushed (Genesis 3:15, note *c*). It was incredibly ironic, therefore, that Jesus—the only perfectly pure soul to come to earth—was lifted up on a cross, or hung on a tree, as if he were accursed. He became the accursed of God for us, suffering the "fierceness of the wrath of Almighty God," and took upon him our sins that we might be forgiven (D&C 76:107; 88:106; Revelation 19:15). Moses was commanded to make a serpent of brass and raise it as a standard with the promise that anyone bitten by the serpents could be healed by looking on it in faith (Numbers 21:4–9). Christ referred to that event as a symbol of his sacrifice for us: "As Moses lifted up the serpent in the wilderness, even so must the Son of man be lifted up: that whosoever believeth in him should not perish, but have eternal life" (John 3:14–15). Some still refused to look because of "the simpleness of the way, or the easiness of it," and they perished (1 Nephi 17:41). Only those who exercise faith in Jesus Christ will have power to "quench all the fiery darts of the wicked" (Ephesians 6:16; D&C 3:8; 27:17).

The scriptures record only seven statements made by the Savior during those nine long, lingering hours on the cross. Interestingly, the word for *seven* in Hebrew is *shevah,* meaning "perfect, whole, complete."

Jesus' first words from the cross were to forgive the soldiers who crucified him (JST Luke 23:35).

His second expression was to extend consoling words to one of the two thieves crucified with him. The first thief reviled Christ as the others had, saying, "If thou art the Christ, save thyself and us" (JST Mark 15:37). "But the [second thief] answering, rebuked [the first], saying, Dost thou not fear God, seeing thou art in the same condemnation? And we indeed justly; for we receive the due reward of our deeds; but this man hath done nothing amiss ['this man is just, and hath not sinned'; JST Matthew 27:47]. And he said to Jesus, Lord, remember me when thou comest into thy kingdom. And Jesus said unto him, Verily I say unto thee; To-day shalt thou be with me in Paradise [the world of spirits]" (JST Luke 23:41–44).[2]

The Savior's third expression was to his mother and to John the Beloved: "When Jesus therefore saw his mother, and the disciple standing by, whom he loved [John the Beloved], he saith unto his mother, Woman, behold thy son! Then saith he to the disciple, Behold thy mother! And from that hour that disciple took her unto his own home" (John 19:26–27). In effect, Jesus was saying to his mother, "We have both known this was to come." Mary had been told by the angel Gabriel, who announced Jesus' birth, that "a spear shall pierce through him to the wounding of thine own soul also" (JST Luke 2:35). When he was a babe in her arms, she must have cuddled him and kissed his face, knowing that she was looking into the face of God. Now the agony she could see etched across his brow broke her heart. How pierced her soul must have been in watching all these events.

By saying to John, "Behold thy mother," Jesus was tenderly committing his mother to John's protective care. Why John? Why not Peter, the presiding authority over the Church, or one of Mary's other children? The Prophet Joseph Smith received a revelation that may help us understand how caring Jesus' choice of John truly was. John the Beloved, John the Revelator, had been promised by Jesus that he would "tarry until I come in my glory" (D&C 7:3). He had been given power over death and would outlive all the other apostles. When Jesus said from the cross, "Behold thy mother!" he may have done so because he knew John was going to outlive her. According to Christian history, Mary spent the rest of her life in John's care. She went with John when Church headquarters was moved from Jerusalem to Ephesus, where she, according to tradition, remained the rest of her life.[3] If that is so, Luke may have met and possibly interviewed her there. Chapter 2 of Luke's account is, apparently, Mary's story as later recounted to Luke, and it has become the real story of Christmas—the most complete account of Jesus' nativity.

DARKNESS PREVAILED

From the sixth hour until the ninth hour (from noon until 6:00 P.M.) there "was a darkness over all the earth. . . . And the sun was darkened" (Luke 23:44–45). When the Light of the world was dying, darkness prevailed in the land. The darkness lasted for three hours in Israel and three days in ancient America (Matthew 27:45; 3 Nephi 8:20–22). During this time the Savior suffered one last traumatic experience. The full weight of the Atonement fell one more time in all its fury. All that Christ had suffered the night before in Gethsemane returned.[4]

Elder Bruce R. McConkie wrote: "All of the anguish, all of the sorrow, and all of the suffering of Gethsemane recurred during the final three hours on the cross, the hours when darkness covered the land. Truly there was no sorrow like unto his sorrow, and no anguish and pain like unto that which bore in with such intensity upon him."[5]

"What happened during those three seemingly endless hours remains outside the bounds of our understanding. Could it be that this was the period of his greatest trial, or that during it the agonies of Gethsemane recurred and even intensified?"[6]

HIS DEATH

"We come now to the last and most terrible irony of Jesus: His feeling forsaken on Calvary at the apogee of His agony."[7] After the Savior had endured nine hours of excruciating pain on the cross, the Father withdrew his Spirit, which evoked the Savior's fourth expression. Elder James E. Talmage has labeled it the greatest soul cry in history:[8] "Eli, Eli, lama sabachthani? that is to say, My God, my God, why hast thou forsaken me?" (Matthew 27:46). The Father had completely withdrawn his Spirit and presence from the Son. The word *Eli* is the more familiar, intimate form of *Elohim*. His words had been recorded many years before in the Twenty-Second Psalm: "My God, my God, why hast thou forsaken me?" (v. 1).

Why would the Father suddenly leave him there alone? The scriptures do not explain why the Father withdrew his Spirit, but prophets and apostles have pondered the possibilities.

Elder Neal A. Maxwell has written: "His suffering—as it were, *enormity* multiplied by *infinity*—evoked His . . . soul-cry on the cross, and it was a cry of forsakenness."[9]

President Brigham Young taught: "God never bestows upon His people, or upon an individual, superior blessings without a severe trial to prove them, to prove that individual, or that people, to see whether they will keep their covenants with Him, and keep in remembrance what He has shown them. Then the greater the vision, the greater the display of the power of the enemy. And when such individuals are off their guard they are left to themselves, as Jesus was. For this express purpose the Father withdrew His spirit from His Son, at the time he was to be crucified. Jesus had been with his Father, talked with Him, dwelt in His bosom, and knew all about heaven, about making the earth, about the transgression of man, and what would redeem the people, and that he was the character who was to redeem the sons of earth, and the earth itself from all sin that had come upon it. The light, knowledge, power, and glory with which he was clothed were far above, or exceeded that of all others who had been upon the earth after the fall, consequently at the very moment, at the hour when the crisis came for him to offer up his life, the Father withdrew Himself, withdrew His Spirit, and cast a vail over him. That is what made him sweat blood. If he had had the power of God upon him, he would not have sweat blood; but all was withdrawn from him, and a veil was cast over him, and he then pled with the Father not to forsake him. 'No,' says the Father, 'you must have your trials, as well as others."[10]

Elder Melvin J. Ballard suggested: "I ask you, what father and mother could stand by and listen to the cry of their children in distress . . . and not render assistance? I have heard of mothers throwing themselves into raging streams when they could not swim a stroke to save their drowning children, [I have heard of fathers] rushing into burning buildings to rescue those whom they loved.

"We cannot stand by and listen to those cries without its touching our hearts. . . . He had the power to save, and He loved His Son, and He could have saved Him. He might have rescued Him from the insult of the crowds. He might have rescued Him when the crown of thorns was placed upon His head. He might have rescued Him when the Son, hanging between two thieves, was mocked with, 'Save thyself, and come down from the cross. He saved others; himself he cannot save.' He listened to all this. He saw that Son condemned; He saw

Him drag the cross through the streets of Jerusalem and faint under its load. He saw the Son finally upon Calvary; he saw His body stretched out upon the wooden cross; He saw the cruel nails driven through hands and feet, and the blows that broke the skin, tore the flesh, and let out the life's blood of His [Only Begotten] Son. . . .

"[He] looked on [all that] with great grief and agony over His Beloved [Child], until there seems to have come a moment when even our Saviour cried out in despair: 'My God, my God, why hast thou forsaken me?'

"In that hour I think I can see our dear Father behind the veil looking upon these dying struggles, . . . His great heart almost breaking for the love that He had for His Son. Oh, in that moment when He might have saved His Son, I thank Him and praise Him that He did not fail us. . . . I rejoice that He did not interfere, and that His love for us made it possible for Him to endure to look upon the sufferings of His [Only Begotten] Son and give Him finally to us, our Saviour and our Redeemer. Without Him, without His sacrifice, we would have remained, and we would never have come glorified into his presence. . . . This is what it cost, in part, for our Father in heaven to give the gift of His Son unto men.

"He, . . . our God, is a jealous God—jealous lest we should [ever] ignore and forget and slight His greatest gift unto us"—the life of his Firstborn Son.[11]

Did Jesus need to know what it was like to be without the Father's Spirit so he would know what it would be like for those who are alienated from God, those from whom the Spirit is withdrawn? He had never been without it. How could he know how to help them? "This deprivation," Elder Maxwell observed, "had never happened to Christ before—never. Yet thereby Jesus became a fully comprehending Christ, and thus He was enabled to be a fully succoring Savior (D&C 88:6; Alma 7:11–12). Moreover, even in the darkest hour, while feeling forsaken, Jesus submitted Himself to the Father . . . [reflecting his] deep, divine determination."[12]

His fifth expression from the cross came shortly thereafter. He simply said, "I thirst" (John 19:28). There was, near the cross, a "vessel full of vinegar, mingled with gall, and they filled a sponge with it, and put upon hyssop, and put to his mouth" (JST John 19:29). The very God who created this world for us, and gave us air and water to sustain our lives, cried out for something to drink. When he thirsted, they had nothing but vinegar to offer him. So ironic. We are often so ungrateful for the blessings he daily showers upon us.

His sixth and seventh expressions from the cross were his last. He cried again with a loud voice, saying, "Father, it is finished, thy will is done" (JST Matthew 27:54). "Father, into thy hands I commend my spirit" (Luke 23:46). Then "he bowed his head, and gave up the ghost" (John 19:30). In other words, his spirit left his body, and his mortal life was over.

At the time of his death, the entire earth convulsed and quaked and trembled (see Matthew 27:51, 54; 3 Nephi 8). When one of the soldiers standing nearby "saw . . . those things that were done," he said, "Truly this was the Son of God" (Matthew 27:54) and "Certainly this was a righteous man" (Luke 23:47). Many of the multitude of disciples who had assembled to see the sight "smote their breasts, and returned" home, grief-stricken and mourning bitterly (Luke 23:48).

When the Savior died, the veil of the temple, which covered the entrance to the Holy of Holies, was "rent in twain from the top to the bottom" (Matthew 27:51). It was as if heaven itself was bearing witness that the veil separating mankind from God had been torn away. Paul suggests that through the rending of the veil of Christ's flesh, we gain entry into the true Holy of Holies, the presence of God (Hebrews 10:19–20).[13] Without Christ's sacrifice, none of us could return to God.

It was late afternoon by now. The Jews urged Pilate to have the soldiers finish the job so that "the bodies should not remain upon the cross on the sabbath day" which began at sunset (John 19:31). They had slain the Lord of the Sabbath but were concerned with their preparations to keep the Sabbath. They "besought Pilate that [the crucified victims'] legs might be broken, and that they might be taken away" (John 19:31). The breaking of the legs hastened death for those hanging on a cross because they could no longer gasp for air by standing on the nail driven through their feet. The soldiers broke the legs of the two thieves, but "when they came to Jesus, and saw that he was dead already, they brake not his legs" (John 19:33). Psalm 34:20 prophetically states: "He keepeth all his bones: not one of them is broken." Since the time of Adam, firstborn male lambs had been offered up as sacrifices without their legs being broken (Exodus 12:46). That too was a type of Christ.

One of the soldiers, observing that Jesus was already dead, pierced his side with a spear, "and forthwith came there out blood and water" (John 19:34). This action fulfilled both a prophecy and a symbol. When Israel was journeying in the wilderness, Moses struck a rock with his staff, and water flowed out to save all Israel from death (Numbers 20). When Christ was struck with a spear, water and blood flowed out, signifying that the "Rock of Israel" had completed the sacrifice and saved us all from spiritual death. Elder James E. Talmage noted that the "blood and water" indicated that the Savior's heart had burst.[14] When he had atoned for the sins of the world, Jesus died of a broken heart and a contrite spirit, having totally submitted to do all the will of his Father. He requires that same offering of us. To be born again and obtain a remission of sin requires us to offer a broken heart and a contrite spirit—a willingness to submit our will to the Father's (3 Nephi 9:20).

Christ fulfilled every type and scriptural promise concerning his first coming and death. The same will be true of his second coming—every promise in the scriptures will be fulfilled: "Yea, all things, every whit, according to the words of the prophets" (3 Nephi 1:20).

BURIAL

When the evening was come, Joseph of Arimathea begged Pilate for the body of Jesus. "Joseph of Arimathea was a man of wealth and station in Jerusalem. We can assume that he had a wide acquaintance and was a man of influence. He was a member of the Sanhedrin, the assembly of seventy-one men constituting the supreme council of the aristocracy which administered the Jewish law."[15]

Nicodemus, who first came to Jesus at night, assisted Joseph of Arimathea. Nicodemus brought "a mixture of myrrh and aloes, about an hundred pound weight" (John 19:39). They wound the Savior's body in clean strips of linen cloth "with the spices, as the manner of the Jews is to bury" (John 19:40; Matthew 27:59). His body was then taken and buried in a tomb just a stone's throw from the site of his crucifixion. The Joseph Smith Translation changes the interpretation of the name *Golgotha* from "place of the skull" to "the place of burial" (JST Matthew 27:35). There, in Joseph's newly hewn tomb, "wherein never man before was laid" (Luke 23:53), the Savior's body was laid to rest. Isaiah had foreseen this event more than seven hundred years earlier: "He made his grave . . . with the rich in his death" (Isaiah 53:9).

Joseph, and presumably Nicodemus, "rolled a great stone" covering the door of the sepulcher and then departed (Matthew 27:60). Friends and family members had "stood afar off, beholding Jesus' crucifixion" (Luke 23:49). The observers included Mary Magdalene, Mary (the Savior's mother), Salome (the mother of Zebedee's children, James, and John), and others (JST Luke 23:56; JST Mark 15:45; JST Matthew 27:59). After they "beheld the sepulchre, and how his body was laid," they returned home to prepare additional burial spices and ointments and to observe the Sabbath day "according to the commandment" (Luke 23:55–56; Mark 15:47).

The next day the chief priests and the Pharisees came together "unto Pilate, saying, Sir, we remember that that deceiver said, while he was yet alive, After three days I will rise again. Command therefore that the sepulchre be made sure until the third day, lest his disciples come by night, and steal him away, and say unto the people, He is risen from the dead" (Matthew 27:62–64).

At the time Jesus prophesied of his resurrection, the chief priests and Pharisees claimed he was blasphemously lying. Now they were afraid of that very possibility. The sepulcher was made sure, the stone was sealed, and guards were posted to stand watch. The greatest miracle in the history of mankind was about to occur.

NOTES

1. The Joseph Smith Translation clarifies that the Savior was forgiving the Roman soldiers; see also Spencer W. Kimball, *Miracle of Forgiveness*, 167.

2. Smith, *Teachings of the Prophet Joseph Smith*, 309.

3. "Introduction to Luke," *Abingdon Bible Commentary*, 1025.

4. Talmage, *Jesus the Christ*, 660–61.

5. McConkie, *Mortal Messiah*, 4:232.

6. Ibid., 4:224–25.

7. Maxwell, *Men and Women of Christ*, 67.

8. Talmage, *Jesus the Christ*, 660–61.

9. Maxwell, "'Willing to Submit,'" 73.

10. Young, *Journal of Discourses*, 3:205–6.

11. Ballard, *Crusader for Righteousness*, 136–38.

12. Maxwell, *Men and Women of Christ*, 67–68.

13. I am indebted to Gerald N. Lund for this insight; see also *Old Testament* [student manual], 154–56.

14. Talmage, *Jesus the Christ*, 668–69; John 19:34.

15. Hunter, Conference Report, October 1960, 107.

IN THE SPIRIT WORLD

They [the righteous] were assembled awaiting the advent of the
Son of God into the spirit world.
—Doctrine and Covenants 138:16

While his body lay in the Garden Tomb at Golgotha (map, page
xii, locations 12 and 11), the Savior entered the postearthly spirit
world. The four Gospels are practically silent regarding the events
that occurred while the Savior's body lay in the tomb. But the scriptures of the Restoration make clear the momentous events of the
Savior's ministry in the spirit world after his crucifixion. Peter
explained that Christ went to the spirit world to proclaim liberty to
the captives and to open the spirit prison to those who were bound,
just as Isaiah had foretold (Isaiah 61:1). Peter said: "For Christ also
once suffered for sins, the just for the unjust, being put to death in
the flesh, but quickened by the Spirit, that he might bring us to God.
For which cause also, he went and preached unto the spirits in
prison; some of whom were disobedient in the days of Noah, while
the long-suffering of God waited, while the ark was preparing,
wherein few, that is, eight souls were saved by water" (JST 1 Peter
3:18–20).

"[He] is ready to judge the quick [living] and the dead. Because of this, is the gospel preached to them who are dead, that they might be judged according to men in the flesh, but live in the spirit according to the will of God" (JST 1 Peter 4:5–6).

Earlier in his mortal ministry, the Savior prophesied about his ministry in the spirit world: "Verily, verily, I say unto you, The hour is coming, and now is, when the dead shall hear the voice of the Son of God; and they who hear shall live. For as the Father hath life in himself, so hath he given to the Son to have life in himself; and hath given him authority to execute judgment also, because he is the Son of man. Marvel not at this; for the hour is coming, in the which all who are in their graves shall hear his voice" (JST John 5:25–28).

The Book of Mormon also relates that while his body lay in the tomb in Jerusalem, the Savior spoke out of the darkness that engulfed the Americas. He did not appear to them at the time but said: "Behold, I am Jesus Christ the Son of God. I created the heavens and the earth, and all things that in them are. I was with the Father from the beginning. I am in the Father, and the Father in me; and in me hath the Father glorified his name. I came unto my own, and my own received me not. And the scriptures concerning my coming are fulfilled. And as many as have received me, to them have I given to become the sons of God; and even so will I to as many as shall believe on my name, for behold, by me redemption cometh" (3 Nephi 9:15–17).

From the teachings of modern prophets we learn the following truths about the spirit world and the Savior's ministry there.

Death provides us entrance into the spirit world and is an important part of the plan for our salvation. At a funeral in 1874, President Brigham Young explained: "What a dark valley and a shadow it is that we call death! To pass from this state of existence as far as the mortal body is concerned, into a state of inanition [emptiness], how strange it is. How dark this valley is. How mysterious is this road, and we have got to travel it alone. I would like to say to you, my friends and brethren, if we could see things as they are, and as we shall see and understand them, this dark shadow and valley is so trifling that we shall turn round and look about upon it and think, when we have crossed it, why this is the greatest advantage of my whole existence, for I have passed from a state of sorrow, grief, mourning, woe, misery, pain, anguish and disappointment into a state of existence, where I can enjoy life to the fullest extent as far as that can be done without a body. My spirit is set free, I thirst no more, I want to sleep no more, I hunger no more, I tire no more, I run, I walk, I labor, I go, I come, I do this, I do that, whatever is required of me, nothing like pain or weariness, I am full of life, full of vigor, and I enjoy the presence of my heavenly Father, by the power of his Spirit. I want to say to my friends, if you will live your religion, live so as to be full of the faith of God, that the light of eternity will shine upon you."[1]

The postearthly spirit world is located on this earth.[2]

The spirit world is where all disembodied spirits have gone from the days of Adam and Eve to the present time where they continue preparing for the resurrection and final judgment.

The spirit world is one world but is divided into spirit paradise and spirit prison.[3] Paradise is described in the scriptures as a place where "those who are righteous are received into a state of happiness, which is called paradise, a state of rest, a state of peace, where they . . . rest from all their troubles and from all care, and sorrow. . . . Thus they remain in this state . . . until the time of their resurrection" (Alma 40:12–14).

The Savior spent three days in the spirit world, teaching and organizing the righteous spirits. Although Peter bore witness that the Savior "preached unto the spirits in prison" (1 Peter 3:19), we learn from modern revelation that he commissioned his disciples in spirit paradise to visit and teach the spirits in prison (D&C 138:28–30). He did not personally appear to those in spirit prison (D&C 138:28–32).

Those in spirit prison have their agency and can choose to accept the message of the gospel. They can repent of sin and exercise faith in God. But to join those in spirit paradise, they also need to have priesthood ordinances performed in their behalf (D&C 138:50–51).[4] These ordinances are performed in temples on the earth by loved ones whose hearts are "turn[ed] to their fathers" (D&C 2:2).

Those who desire to leave spirit prison and enter the realms of the righteous in spirit paradise face three important requirements: first, they must accept the gospel of Jesus Christ with all their hearts; second, they must repent of their sins; and third, they must have priesthood ordinances performed in their behalf by those living on the earth.[5]

In 1918, President Joseph F. Smith received a revelation about what the Savior did while he was in the spirit world. At the time the revelation was given, President Smith's health was failing. In the October general conference, just six weeks before his death, he said: "As most of you, I suppose, are aware, I have been undergoing a siege of very serious illness for the last five months. It would be impossible for me, on this occasion, to occupy sufficient time to express the desires of my heart and my feelings, as I would desire to express them to you, but I felt that it was my duty, if possible, to be present. . . .

" . . . Although somewhat weakened in body, my mind is clear with reference to my duty, and with reference to the duties and responsibilities that rest upon the Latter-day Saints; and I am ever anxious for the progress of the work of the Lord, for the prosperity of the people of the Church of Jesus Christ of Latter-day Saints throughout the world. . . .

"I will not, I dare not, attempt to enter upon many things that are resting upon my mind this morning, and I shall postpone until some future time, the Lord being willing, my attempt to tell you some of the things that are in my mind, and that dwell in my heart. I have not lived alone these five months. I have dwelt in the spirit of prayer, of supplication, of faith and of determination; and I have had my communication with the Spirit of the Lord continuously."[6]

Two weeks later, President Smith asked his son Elder Joseph Fielding Smith to record the vision he had been shown about the spirit world. President Smith's vision is the most detailed account we have of where the Savior was and what he did during the three days his body lay in the tomb (D&C 138). From it we learn that Christ entered spirit paradise where the righteous are but did not go personally among the wicked. He "organized his forces and appointed messengers, clothed with power and authority, and commissioned them to go forth and carry the light of the gospel to them that were in darkness, even to all the spirits of men; and thus was the gospel preached to the dead" (D&C 138:30). Thus, the Savior bridged the gulf between the righteous and the wicked, between paradise and spirit prison.

In a revelation to the Prophet Joseph Smith, the Lord revealed that all who live on earth at times and in circumstances that prevented them from hearing the message of Jesus Christ will have an opportunity to hear and accept the gospel in the spirit world: "Thus came the voice of the Lord unto me, saying: All who have died without a knowledge of this gospel, who would have received it if they had been permitted to tarry, shall be heirs of the celestial kingdom of God; also all that shall die henceforth without a knowledge of it, who would have received it with all their hearts, shall be heirs of that kingdom; for I, the Lord, will judge all men according to their works, according to the desire of their hearts" (D&C 137:7–9).

Doesn't this doctrine make perfect sense? Any plan of salvation claiming to come from God would have to include provisions for all of his children. Why would he preclude any of them? The performance of proxy (vicarious) ordinances for deceased loved ones is essential to salvation. The Prophet Joseph Smith said that the work done in temples is the "most glorious of all subjects belonging to the everlasting gospel" (D&C 128:17). Our ancestors are depending on us to do their temple work. They cannot do it for themselves.

"And now, my dearly beloved brethren and sisters, let me assure you that these are principles in relation to the dead and the living that cannot be lightly passed over, as pertaining to our salvation. For their salvation is necessary and essential to our salvation, as Paul says concerning the fathers—that they without us cannot be made perfect—neither can we without our dead be made perfect.

" . . . for Malachi says, last chapter, verses 5th and 6th: Behold, I will send you Elijah the prophet before the coming of the great and dreadful day of the Lord: And he shall turn the heart of the fathers to the children, and the heart of the children to their fathers, lest I come and smite the earth with a curse.

" . . . It is sufficient to know . . . that the earth will be smitten with a curse unless there is a welding link of some kind or other between the fathers and the children, upon some subject or other—and behold what is that subject? It is the baptism for the dead. For we without them cannot be made perfect; neither can they without us be made perfect" (D&C 128:15–18).

They cannot be made perfect without receiving the ordinances that can only be performed on this earth. And we cannot be made perfect unless we do that work. President Gordon B. Hinckley said, "This work, unselfishly given in behalf of those on the other side, comes nearer to the unparalleled vicarious work of the Savior than any other of which I know. The great and important work of teaching the gospel of Christ to the people of the world is incomplete, at best, if it does not also provide for that teaching to those in another sphere and making available to them those gospel ordinances required of all if they are to move forward on the way to eternal life."[7]

Temple ordinances for the deceased are so important that divine help has been sent on many occasions to encourage or assist us in this work. We may not have "beyond the veil" experiences, but those involved in family history work often have "near the veil" experiences. Following is an account of one Latter-day Saint who learned the necessity of temple work from those beyond the veil that separates us from our deceased loved ones.

Frederick William Hurst and his brother Charles were New Zealanders who were baptized into the Church in Australia in 1854 and later emigrated to Utah. In 1875, they were called to return to New Zealand as missionaries, where they tried to share the restored gospel with the rest of their family, but their efforts were rejected. No other family members ever joined the Church. Of this experience Frederick wrote, "My heart was so sore I could not forbear shedding tears." In 1892, he was called upon to use his talents as an artist, helping to engrave and paint the interior of the Salt Lake Temple. Although he was very ill at the time and "so sick with vomiting," he believed the completion of the temple was of such importance that he never missed a day's work until the project was finished. One of his last journal entries is a truly remarkable one and a testimony of the importance of family history and temple work to every individual. Frederick recorded:

"Along about the 1st of March, 1893, I found myself alone in the dining room, all had gone to bed. I was sitting at the table when to my great surprise my elder brother Alfred walked in and sat down opposite me at the table and smiled. I said to him (he looked so natural): 'When did you arrive in Utah?'

"He said: 'I have just come from the Spirit World, this is not my body that you see, it is lying in the tomb. I want to tell you that when you were on you[r] mission you told me many things about the Gospel, and the hereafter, and about the Spirit World being as real and tangible as the earth. I could not believe you, but when I died and went there and saw for myself I realized that you had told the truth. I attended the Mormon meetings.' He raised his hand and said with much warmth: 'I believe in the Lord Jesus Christ with all my heart. I believe in faith, and repentance and baptism for the remission of sins, but that is as far as I can go. I look to you to do the work for me in the temple. . . . We are all looking to you as our head in this great work.'"[8] He accordingly arranged for the temple work to be done.

The ongoing preaching of the gospel in the spirit world and the increased temple building on the earth bear witness that the Savior's atonement and resurrection saves both the living and the dead. As we do temple work for deceased ancestors, we should know that what happens in temples really does have an effect on them. Elder Rudger Clawson, an apostle, learned that truth through the following experience:

"Some years ago, a brother approached me, and he said: 'Brother Clawson, I am sixty-seven years of age; I have been a strong and active man in my life, and have done a great deal of hard work, but now I am somewhat feeble; I can not engage in manual labor as heretofore. How shall I spend my time?' I said to him, 'Go to the house of the Lord.' 'Thank you,' he replied, 'I will take your counsel.' About eight years later, I met this brother again. He appeared to be very happy indeed; and there was an expression of joy in his countenance. 'Brother Clawson,' he said, 'during the past eight years

I have been working for my ancestors, in the house of the Lord. After that conversation with you, I went east and I gathered up eight hundred names of my relatives; and during the past eight years I have personally officiated for three hundred of my ancestors, and I propose to continue on with the good work; I am happy for the Lord has blessed me.' He further said, 'I saw in vision, upon one occasion, my father and mother, who were not members of the Church, who had not received the Gospel in life, and I discovered that they were living separate and apart in the spirit world, and when I asked them how it was that they were so, my father said: "This is an enforced separation, and you are the only individual that can bring us together; you can do this work; will you do it?"' . . . and he informed me that he had attended to the work, and I rejoiced with him and congratulated him."⁹

Temple and family history work can bind generations together, heart to heart, so that "that same sociality which exists among us here will exist among us" in the eternities (D&C 130:2). Temple work is but the grand extension of the Savior's ministry in the spirit world.

After his three-day ministry in the spirit world while his body lay in the tomb, the greatest miracle ever performed on this earth occurred: Christ rose from the dead.

NOTES

1. Young, *Deseret News Semi-Weekly,* 28 July 1874, 1, cited in *Brigham Young,* 273.
2. Young, *Journal of Discourses,* 3:369, 372.
3. Smith, *Doctrines of Salvation,* 2:230.
4. Smith, *Gospel Doctrine,* 438; Smith, *Doctrines of Salvation,* 2:158.
5. Smith, *Gospel Doctrine,* 438; Smith, *Doctrines of Salvation,* 2:158.
6. Smith, Conference Report, October 1918, 2.
7. Hinckley, "Rejoice in This Great Era of Temple Building," 56.
8. Devitry-Smith, "The Saint and the Grave Robber," 40, 42.
9. Clawson, Conference Report, October 1908, 74.

THE RESURRECTION AND REUNION WITH THE FATHER 9

He is risen; he is not here.
—*JST Mark 16:4*

On Sunday morning, the first day of the week, just as the sun was rising, Mary Magdalene and the other women came to the sepulcher with sweet spices to anoint the Savior's body. A new day was dawning in the history of the world. For most Christians, from this moment on, Sunday would be the day of worship as a reminder of the sweet blessing of Christ's resurrection.

As they approached the tomb, they could see the large stone had been rolled away. Mary immediately assumed his body had been stolen. She ran to tell Peter and John.

The other women, however, saw that there were "two angels standing by it in shining garments ['long white garments'; JST Mark 16:3]. . . . They were much perplexed thereabout; and were affrighted, and bowed down their faces to the earth" (JST Luke 24:2–4). The guards at the tomb were struck with so much fear that they fell to the earth "as though they were dead" (JST Matthew 28:3).

The angels made a startling announcement: "We know that ye seek Jesus who was crucified. He is not here; for he is risen, as he said" (JST Matthew 28:4–5).

The angels continued: "Behold the place where they laid him. . . . And they, entering into the sepulcher, saw the place where they laid Jesus" (JST Mark 16:4–6). "And go quickly, and tell his disciples that he is risen from the dead; and, behold, he goeth before you into Galilee; there shall ye see him" (Matthew 28:7).

No greater announcement has ever been made. The first person to rise from the dead as a resurrected being had risen! The world, with all its wisdom, had never attained the power to resurrect one single soul. The resurrection is the work of God, and now, because of Christ, all mankind would be able to experience its blessings. "Without the Resurrection," Elder Howard W. Hunter taught, "the gospel of Jesus Christ becomes a litany of wise sayings and seemingly unexplainable miracles . . . with no ultimate triumph. No, the ultimate triumph is in the ultimate miracle. . . . [Jesus'] triumph over physical and spiritual death is the good news every Christian tongue should speak."[1]

The women quickly ran back to the city to tell the apostles, who at first did not know what to think: "And their words seemed to them as idle tales, and they believed them not" (Luke 24:11). When the guards later reported to the chief priests "all the things that were done," the chief priests called a council and conspired to bribe the guards to say, "His disciples came by night, and stole him away while we slept" (Matthew 28:11–13).

While the other women were running to tell the apostles the news, Mary went to find Peter and John. She exclaimed, "They have taken away the Lord out of the sepulchre, and we know not where they have laid him" (John 20:2). Peter and John ran as fast as they could to the tomb. John outran Peter, arriving at the tomb first. John looked in and saw the burial clothes but did not enter (John 20:4–5). When Peter arrived he went in first (John 20:6) and "beheld the linen clothes laid by themselves" (Luke 24:12). He saw "the napkin, that was about his head, not lying with the linen clothes, but wrapped together in a place by itself" (John 20:7). John then joined Peter in the sepulcher, where he also saw the burial napkin folded neatly and lying in a place by itself: "he saw, and believed" (John 20:8).

What was it about a folded burial napkin that convinced them Jesus had indeed been resurrected and not stolen? No thief would have taken time to fold the burial clothing. Not in that tomb, that morning. Jesus arose from the dead and folded his own burial clothes. And because he did, we can all do the same.[2] One day we will rise from the dead and go on to eternal life, only because of his power over death. Every time we leave the temple, having folded up the clothing that one day we will be buried in, we can ponder the significance of his resurrection and be grateful for what he did.

Shortly after Peter and John had left the sepulcher, Mary arrived back at the Garden Tomb. She was weeping, not knowing what the others knew. She looked into the sepulcher and saw the two angels who had made the earlier announcement (John 20:11–12). They asked her, "Woman, why weepest thou? She saith unto them, Because they have taken away my Lord, and I know not where they have laid him. And when she had thus said, she turned herself back, and saw Jesus standing, and knew not that it was Jesus.

"Jesus saith unto her, Woman, why weepest thou? whom seekest thou? She, supposing him to be the gardener, saith unto him, Sir, if thou have borne him hence, tell me where thou hast laid him, and I will take him away.

"Jesus saith unto her, Mary. She turned herself, and saith unto him, Rabboni; which is to say, Master" (John 20:13–16).

The Joseph Smith Translation and other translations of the Bible may seem to indicate that she embraced the Savior.[3] But, whether she embraced him or not, Mary was the first mortal to see the resurrected Lord. At some point the Savior indicated to Mary that it was time for him to leave. She obviously did not want him to go. He said, "Hold me not; for I am not yet ascended to my Father; but go to my brethren, and say unto them, I ascend unto my Father, and your Father; and to my God, and your God. Mary Magdalene [then] came and told the disciples that she had seen the Lord, and that he had spoken these things unto her" (JST John 20:17–18).

Can you imagine what it must have been like for God, who had to leave his Son alone without his Spirit on the cross three days earlier, now to greet him? What must this reunion between the Father and the Son have been like? How great was their anticipation to see one another and be with one another again? When they met, how long would they have embraced? How long would it have been before the Father spoke? And what could he have said to his Beloved Son to express his immense love?

Can you picture in your mind's eye the reuniting of the Father with his Son? Can you hear the Savior declare, "Father, thy will has been done, and the glory be thine forever"? That is precisely what the Atonement makes possible: a reuniting with the Father. Because of what Christ did for us in his final hours, it is now possible for all mankind—every one who so desires—to return to the Father's presence. The reunion in the resurrection will include families and friends, but most important, it will be a reunion with our Eternal Father. Our Father in Heaven, like the father in the parable of the prodigal son, looks forward to our return. He stands ready, with open arms, to greet us.

Elder Jeffrey R. Holland once observed a reunion at an airport between a missionary son and a father that seemed beautifully reminiscent of what this marvelous reunion between the Eternal Father and his own Beloved Son must surely have been like, only that reunion was multiplied by more unreserved love than has probably ever been expressed or experienced in all eternity between any father and son. Elder Holland exclaimed, "Even in my limited imagination I can see that reunion in the heavens. And I pray for one like it for you and for me. I pray for reconciliation and for forgiveness, for mercy, and for the Christian growth and Christian character we must develop if we are to enjoy such a moment fully."[4]

THE REALITY OF CHRIST'S RESURRECTION

There are many eyewitnesses for the literal resurrection of our Lord and Savior. That event is the most verified event in all scripture.

John the Beloved declared, "These are written, that ye might believe that Jesus is the Christ, the Son of God; and that believing ye might have life through his name" (John 20:31). Many Saints arose at the time of Christ's resurrection and went into the city of Jerusalem and appeared unto many (Matthew 27:52–53). All the righteous dead from Adam's day to the Savior's day were resurrected with him (Mosiah 15:21). The people in the Book of Mormon were told by Samuel the Lamanite prophet the same message—that many would arise from the dead, appear unto them, and minister to them at the time of the Savior's resurrection—and they did (3 Nephi 23:11).

Following is a brief summary of the eyewitness accounts:

Jesus appeared to Mary Magdalene at the Garden Tomb (John 20:1–18).

Jesus appeared to the other women (Matthew 28:9–10).

Jesus appeared to two disciples on the road to Emmaus (Luke 24:13–52).

Jesus appeared to Peter (Luke 24:34; 1 Corinthians 15:5).

Jesus appeared to the apostles without Thomas being present (Luke 24:34–39).

Jesus appeared to the apostles with Thomas present (John 20:26–29).

Jesus appeared to seven of his disciples at the Sea of Tiberias (John 21:1–19).

Jesus appeared to his apostles at the Sea of Galilee (Matthew 28:16–20).

Jesus appeared to more than five hundred brethren (1 Corinthians 15:6).

Jesus appeared to and instructed the apostles for forty days and "showed himself alive" among them with "many infallible proofs" (Acts 1:3).

Jesus walked with the eleven apostles to the top of the Mount of Olives and as far as Bethany on the other side, blessed them, and then ascended into heaven (Luke 24:49–53). "Two men . . . in white apparel" declared, "Ye men of Galilee, why stand ye gazing up into heaven? this same Jesus, which is taken up from you into heaven, shall so come in like manner as ye have seen him go into heaven" (Acts 1:10–11).

Others besides those in the Bible have seen the resurrected Lord. They also stand as witnesses of his literal resurrection from the dead:

Jesus appeared to twenty-five hundred people at the temple in the land Bountiful (3 Nephi 17:25) who each, one by one, felt for themselves the prints in his hands and feet (3 Nephi 11:15). He declared to these people, "Behold . . . I have laid down my life, and have taken it up again; therefore repent, and come unto me ye ends of the earth, and be saved" (3 Nephi 9:22). He remained for three days teaching even larger groups (3 Nephi 19:1–3).

Jesus and the Father appeared to Joseph Smith in the Sacred Grove, in Palmyra, New York (Joseph Smith–History 1:16–20).

Jesus appeared to Joseph Smith and Sidney Rigdon in Hiram, Ohio. They said: "This is the testimony . . . which we give of him: That he lives! For we saw him" (D&C 76:22–23).

Jesus appeared to Joseph Smith and Oliver Cowdery in the Kirtland Temple (D&C 110). Their description of the power and glory attending the risen Christ ranks among the most beautiful ever penned by any of the prophets (D&C 110:1–10).

Jesus has appeared to many in the latter days. Their testimonies may be unrecorded for the world to look upon, but the quiet certitude manifest in their lives bears witness that the resurrection is real. They can say with Job, "For I know that my redeemer liveth, and that he shall stand at the latter day upon the earth" (Job 19:25).

The resurrection is the crowning event of the Atonement. Christ's resurrection forever broke the bands of physical death for all mankind and guaranteed every person immortality. Because of him death holds no fear. As Lehi exclaimed to his family: "Wherefore, how great the importance to make these things known unto the inhabitants of the earth, that they may know that there is no flesh that can dwell in the presence of God, save it be through the merits, and mercy, and grace of the Holy Messiah, who layeth down his life according to the flesh, and taketh it again by the power of the Spirit, that he may bring to pass the resurrection of the dead, being the first that should rise" (2 Nephi 2:8).

In the resurrection, the blessings of God will be so great that we will no longer worry about any of the trials we endured in mortality: "God shall wipe away all tears from their eyes; and there shall be no more death, neither sorrow, nor crying, neither shall there be any more pain: for the former things are passed away" (Revelation 21:4).

The Prophet Joseph Smith taught: "All your losses will be made up to you in the resurrection, provided you continue faithful. By the vision of the Almighty I have seen it."[5]

President Lorenzo Snow testified of the physical blessings the resurrection bestows: "The prospects that have been opened up to us are grand. In the next life we will have our bodies glorified and free from sickness and death. Nothing is so beautiful as a person in a resurrected and glorified condition. There is nothing more lovely than to be in this condition and have our wives and children and friends with us."[6]

President Brigham Young also described the incredible miracle of the resurrection and the great blessings that are ours because of it: "Those who attain to the blessing of the first or celestial resurrection will be pure and holy, and perfect in body. Every man and woman that reaches to this unspeakable attainment will be as beautiful as the angels that surround the throne of God. If you can, by faithfulness in this life, obtain the right to come up in the morning of the resurrection, you need entertain no fears that the wife will be dissatisfied with her husband, or the husband with the wife; for those of the first resurrection will be free from sin and from the consequences and power of sin."[7]

The words to one of our soul-stirring hymns bear a beautiful testimony of the Savior's resurrection and the confidence it gives to all who believe:

> *I know that my Redeemer lives.*
> *What comfort this sweet sentence gives!*
> *He lives, he lives, who once was dead.*
> *He lives, my ever-living Head.*
> *He lives to bless me with his love.*

He lives to plead for me above.
He lives my hungry soul to feed.
He lives to bless in time of need.

He lives to grant me rich supply.
He lives to guide me with his eye.
He lives to comfort me when faint.
He lives to hear my soul's complaint.
He lives to silence all my fears.
He lives to wipe away my tears.
He lives to calm my troubled heart.
He lives all blessings to impart.

He lives, my kind, wise heav'nly Friend.
He lives and loves me to the end.
He lives, and while he lives, I'll sing.
He lives, my Prophet, Priest, and King.
He lives and grants me daily breath.
He lives, and I shall conquer death.
He lives my mansion to prepare.
He lives to bring me safely there.

He lives! All glory to his name!
He lives, my Savior, still the same.
Oh, sweet the joy this sentence gives:
"I know that my Redeemer lives!"[8]

NOTES

1. Hunter, Conference Report, April 1986, 18.
2. I am indebted to Gerald N. Lund for this insight.
3. Joseph Smith's translation of John 20:17 reads "hold me not" rather than "touch me not." See also the *New International Version Study Bible,* which translates this phrase as "Do not hold on to me," implying that she would not let him go.
4. Holland, "I Stand All Amazed," 72–73.
5. Smith, *Teachings of the Prophet Joseph Smith,* 296.
6. Snow, Conference Report, October 1900, 63.
7. Young, *Journal of Discourses,* 10:24.
8. *Hymns,* no. 136.

"THOU HAST DONE WONDERFUL THINGS" 10

His name shall be called Wonderful.
—*Isaiah 9:6*

The inner peace emanating from knowing Christ and having had a witness borne of the Spirit about the Atonement surpasses all understanding. In Lehi's incredible dream of the tree of life (1 Nephi 8), the central figure and the most important symbol was the tree. Christ is the tree of life, which represents the love of God (1 Nephi 11:4–6, 25). Christ invites us to partake of the Atonement (the fruit of the tree), which he has promised is sweet above all that is sweet, white above all that is white, even exceeding the whiteness of the driven snow, desirable above all other fruit, offering beauty that exceeds all beauty, being pure above all that is pure, and most joyous to the soul (1 Nephi 8:11–12; 11:8–9, 23). In other words, the blessings of the Atonement eclipse everything we have ever seen, heard of, or imagined in this life (1 Corinthians 2:9; D&C 133:45). It is the greatest of all the gifts of God (1 Nephi 15:36). Partaking of it will make us happy (1 Nephi 8:10) and fill us with a desire to share that gift with

everyone we know (1 Nephi 8:13–17; Alma 36:24). There is simply
nothing on this earth or in all human history to compare with what
Christ did for us in his final hours. "To ignore him," Dr. Robert J.
Matthews taught, "is the greatest form of ingratitude. To fail to obey
him is the greatest of all mistakes. To follow him and to serve him is
the greatest happiness."[1]

Our debt to him is so enormous that no effort on our part will
ever put him in our debt: "In the first place, he hath created you, and
granted unto you your lives, for which ye are indebted unto him.
And secondly, he doth require that ye should do as he hath commanded you; for which if ye do, he doth immediately bless you; and
therefore he hath paid you. And ye are still indebted unto him, and
are, and will be, forever and ever; therefore, of what have ye to
boast?" (Mosiah 2:23–24).

Although we can never boast of our offerings to God, we can,
nonetheless, be magnified by our efforts to make those offerings. An
analogy of how that works was described by Elder James E. Talmage
in "The Parable of the Grateful Cat":

"A certain English student of Natural History, as I have heard,
once upon a time had the [following] experience . . .

"Mr. Romanes, in the course of his customary daily walk, came to
a mill-pond. At the edge of the water he saw two boys with a basket.
They were obviously engaged in a diverting occupation. As he came
up to them Mr. Romanes observed that the youths were well dressed
and evidently somewhat refined and cultured. Inquiry elicited the
fact that they were upper servants in a family of wealth and social
quality. In the basket were three whining kittens; two others were
drowning in the pond; and the mother cat was running about on the
bank, rampant in her distress.

"To the naturalist's inquiry the boys responded with a straight-
forward statement, respectfully addressed. They said their mistress
had instructed them to drown the kittens, as she wanted no other cat
than the old one about the house. The mother cat, as the boys
explained, was the lady's particular pet. Mr. Romanes assured the
boys that he was a personal friend of their employer, and that he
would be responsible for any apparent dereliction in their obedience

to the orders of their mistress. He gave the boys a shilling apiece, and took the three living kittens in charge. The two in the pond had already sunk to their doom.

"The mother cat evinced more than the measure of intelligence usually attributed to the animal world. She recognized the man as the deliverer of her three children, who but for him would have been drowned. As he carried the kittens she trotted along—sometimes following, sometimes alongside, occasionally rubbing against him with grateful yet mournful purrs. At his home Mr. Romanes provided the kittens with comfortable quarters, and left the mother cat in joyful content. She seemed to have forgotten the death of the two in her joy over the rescue of the three.

"Next day, the gentleman was seated in his parlor on the ground floor, in the midst of a notable company. Many people had gathered to do honor to the distinguished naturalist. The cat came in. In her mouth she carried a large, fat mouse, not dead, but still feebly struggling under the pains of torturous capture. She laid her panting and well-nigh expiring prey at the feet of the man who had saved her kittens.

"What think you of the offering, and of the purpose that prompted the act? A live mouse, fleshy and fat! Within the cat's power of possible estimation and judgment it was a superlative gift. To her limited understanding no rational creature could feel otherwise than pleased over the present of a meaty mouse. Every sensible cat would be ravenously joyful with such an offering. Beings unable to appreciate a mouse for a meal were unknown to the cat.

"Are not our offerings to the Lord . . . as thoroughly unnecessary to His needs as was the mouse to the scientist? But remember that the grateful and sacrificing nature of the cat was enlarged, and in a measure sanctified, by her offering.

"Thanks be to God that He gauges the offerings and sacrifices of His children by the standard of their physical ability and honest intent rather than by the gradation of His exalted station. Verily He is God with us; and He both understands and accepts our motives and righteous desires. Our need to serve God is incalculably greater than His need for our service."[2]

God truly does appreciate our efforts, regardless of how small they may be. He is so gracious that he responds to even our smallest sacrifices with outpourings of infinite love. He recognized the immense sacrifice made by a widow and honored her for her efforts (Mark 12:42–44). He praised Oliver Granger, an early Church member who later lost most of his eyesight and died serving the Lord to the best of his ability: "His sacrifice shall be more sacred unto me than his increase. . . . Let the blessings of my people be on him forever and ever" (D&C 117:13–15).

The Savior purchased our eternal lives with such a tremendous price. Will it ever be possible for us, weak mortals that we are, to comprehend fully the magnitude of what he offers us? Can we ever show enough gratitude and appreciation? It may be beyond our ability to comprehend how the Savior took upon himself all the sins of mankind in Gethsemane and on the cross, but it is not beyond our capacity to pay tribute to the Father and the Son for what was done. We may not fully understand the Lord's blessings to us or how the Atonement was accomplished, but we do know why, and we can be grateful.

SHOWING GRATITUDE TO GOD

Through his holy prophets and the scriptures, God has kindly revealed ways we can express gratitude to him.

Serve others. We obtain the blessings of the Atonement through repentance and receiving the ordinances of the gospel; we retain these blessings by being humble (Mosiah 4:11–12) and by serving others as he would if he were there: "For the sake of retaining a remission of your sins from day to day, that ye may walk guiltless before God—I would that ye should impart of your substance to the poor, every man according to that which he hath, such as feeding the hungry, clothing the naked, visiting the sick and administering to their relief, both spiritually and temporally, according to their wants [needs]" (Mosiah 4:26; James 1:27; Alma 34:28–29). "I tell you these things that ye may learn wisdom; that ye may learn that when ye are in the service of your fellow beings ye are only in the service of your God" (Mosiah 2:17). "Inasmuch as ye have done it [good deeds and acts of kindness] unto one of the least of these my brethren, ye have done it unto me" (Matthew 25:40).

Give thanks. An attitude of gratitude tells God we love and appreciate him: "Render all the thanks and praise which your whole soul has power to possess, to that God who has created you, and has kept and preserved you" (Mosiah 2:20). "Let all thy thoughts be directed unto the Lord; yea, let the affections of thy heart be placed upon the Lord forever. Counsel with the Lord in all thy doings, and he will direct thee for good; yea, when thou liest down at night lie down unto the Lord, that he may watch over you in your sleep; and when thou risest in the morning let thy heart be full of thanks unto God; and if ye do these things, ye shall be lifted up at the last day" (Alma 37:36–37).

Keep his commandments. It is an act of intelligence and wisdom to keep God's commandments (Alma 37:35–36; D&C 93:36–37, 39–40). Few other things will help us grow closer to God than strict obedience to the commandments. When we yield to sin, through fear or abandonment of principles, we lose blessings. Obedience brings blessings in this life and "advantage[s] in the world to come" (D&C 130:19).

Show reverence. True spirituality includes humility and respect for sacred things (D&C 63:64). Reverence can never be compelled. It is a gift we give with sincere and heartfelt appreciation. It is an outgrowth of our humility before God. "The greatest manifestation of spirituality is reverence; indeed, reverence is spirituality. Reverence is profound respect mingled with love."[3] Such profound respect for God and for the atoning sacrifice of Jesus Christ leads us to look deep into our hearts. It fills us with a desire never to do anything that would distract others from the Spirit or from coming unto him (D&C 88:69, 121).

Light-mindedness, in contrast to lightmindedness, leads us to reverence. The Prophet Joseph Smith wisely observed: "A fanciful and flowery and heated imagination beware of; because the things of God are of deep import; and time, and experience, and careful and ponderous and solemn thoughts can only find them out. Thy mind, O man! if thou wilt lead a soul unto salvation, must stretch as high as the utmost heavens, and search into and contemplate the darkest abyss, and the broad expanse of eternity—thou must commune with God. How much more dignified and noble are the thoughts of God, than the vain imaginations of the human heart!"[4] Pride, vanity, and self-aggrandizement or self-promotion all run contrary to the cardinal virtues of humility and reverence.

"GREATER LOVE HATH NO MAN"

Our Father and the Savior love us with greater love than we can comprehend. Their whole desire and effort is to help us become as they are and return to their presence. Their love for us is overwhelming. We feel it on occasions in mortal life, but we will experience it in even greater ways at the Day of Judgment. The Savior declared that at that day he will plead for us and bless us: "Listen to him who is the advocate with the Father, who is pleading your cause before him—saying: Father, behold the sufferings and death of him who did no sin, in whom thou wast well pleased; behold the blood of thy Son which was shed, the blood of him whom thou gavest that thyself might be glorified; wherefore, Father, spare these my brethren that believe on my name, that they may come unto me and have everlasting life" (D&C 45:3–5).

The Savior not only pleads with the Father on our behalf but has the power to help and heal us. We are not beyond his ability or his desire to help. Elder Boyd K. Packer testified: "Restoring what you cannot restore, healing the wound you cannot heal, fixing that which you broke and you cannot fix is the very purpose of the atonement of Christ.

"When your desire is firm and you are willing to pay the 'uttermost farthing,' the law of restitution is suspended. Your obligation is transferred to the Lord. He will settle your accounts.

"I repeat, save for the exception of the very few who defect to perdition, there is no habit, no addiction, no rebellion, no transgression, no apostasy, no crime exempted from the promise of complete forgiveness. That is the promise of the atonement of Christ."[5]

President J. Reuben Clark Jr. tried to help us understand how real His mercy and love will be at the Day of Judgment: "I believe that

the Lord will help us. I believe if we go to him he will give us understanding, if we are living righteously. I believe he will answer our
prayers. I believe that our Heavenly Father wants to save every one of
his children. I do not think he intends to shut any of us off because
of some slight transgression, some slight failure to observe some rule
or regulation. There are the great elementals that we must observe,
but he is not going to be captious about the lesser things.

"I believe that his juridical concept of his dealings with his children could be expressed in this way: I believe that in his justice and
mercy he will give us the maximum reward for our acts, give us all
that he can give, and in the reverse, I believe that he will impose upon
us the minimum penalty which it is possible for him to impose."[6]

EVERY KNEE SHALL BOW

All that Christ has passed through will one day cause every knee
to bow in deep and humble gratitude. We will then, if not before,
gladly kneel in adoration and thank him for working through the
great atonement and thank the Father for his glorious plan for our
salvation. How long will we go on thanking him? John the Revelator
declared: "Unto him who loved us, be glory; who washed us from our
sins in his own blood, and hath made us kings and priests unto God,
his Father. To him be glory and dominion, forever and ever" (JST
Revelation 1:6). "All knees shall bow in His presence," Elder Maxwell
wrote, "and all tongues confess His name. (See D&C 76:110–11;
Philip. 2:10–11.) Knees which never before have assumed that pos-
ture for that purpose will do so then—and promptly. Tongues which
have never before spoken His name except in gross profanity will do
so then—and worshipfully. . . . All will then acknowledge the com-
pleteness of His justice and His mercy (see Alma 12:15) and will see
how human indifference to God—not God's indifference to
humanity—accounts for so much suffering."[7]

The feeling of love generated by our realization of what he did for
us will be as intense and inexpressible as the appreciation of the
Nephites who saw him when he appeared in ancient America: "And
when [Jesus] had said these words, he himself also knelt upon the
earth; and behold he prayed unto the Father, and the things which

he prayed cannot be written. . . . And no tongue can speak, neither can there be written by any man, neither can the hearts of men conceive so great and marvelous things as we both saw and heard Jesus speak; and no one can conceive of the joy which filled our souls at the time we heard him pray for us unto the Father" (3 Nephi 17:15–17).

"THOU HAST DONE WONDERFUL THINGS"

Isaiah exclaimed, "O Lord, thou art my God; I will exalt thee, I will praise thy name; for thou hast done wonderful things" (Isaiah 25:1). The Savior opened the door to Heavenly Father's presence for all of God's children (Isaiah 22:22). Nowhere is this truth expressed more beautifully than in the Book of Mormon:

"He doeth not anything save it be for the benefit of the world; for he loveth the world, even that he layeth down his own life that he may draw all men unto him. Wherefore, he commandeth none that they shall not partake of his salvation.

"Behold, doth he cry unto any, saying: Depart from me? Behold, I say unto you, Nay; but he saith: Come unto me all ye ends of the earth, buy milk and honey, without money and without price.

"Behold, hath he commanded any that they should depart out of the synagogues, or out of the houses of worship? Behold, I say unto you, Nay.

"Hath he commanded any that they should not partake of his salvation? Behold I say unto you, Nay; but he hath given it free for all men; and he hath commanded his people that they should persuade all men to repentance.

"Behold, hath the Lord commanded any that they should not partake of his goodness? Behold I say unto you, Nay; but all men are privileged the one like unto the other, and none are forbidden. . . .

" . . . For he doeth that which is good among the children of men; and he doeth nothing save it be plain unto the children of men; and he inviteth them all to come unto him and partake of his goodness; and he denieth none that come unto him, black and white, bond and free, male and female; and he remembereth the heathen; and all are alike unto God, both Jew and Gentile" (2 Nephi 26:24–33).

Besides opening the door to eternal life, the Savior is the source of spiritual strength. He is our eternal Hope and our immediate Help:

He is a strength during times of trial (Isaiah 25:1–4; 32:1–2).

He is a refuge from the storms of life (Isaiah 25:4).

He is a shadow from the heat of the deserts of despair that surround us (Isaiah 25:4).

He is a hiding place from the winds of adversity that blow against us (Isaiah 32:2).

He is a covert (cover) from the tempests that billow and surge around us (Isaiah 32:2).

He is rivers of water in the dry places, the wildernesses we travel through (Isaiah 32:2).

He is the shadow of a great rock to protect us from the spiritually desolate lands we live in (Isaiah 32:2).

He wipes away all tears from our eyes (Isaiah 25:8; Revelation 21:4).

He is our sure foundation upon which, if we build, we shall never fall (Isaiah 28:16; Helaman 5:12; D&C 50:44).

He knows our trials and directs our paths (Isaiah 30:19–21).

Knowing all these things about Christ, Isaiah occasionally bursts into hymns of praise in his writings. Some of these have been immortalized in our hearts and modern anthems: "For unto us a child is born, unto us a son is given: and the government shall be upon his shoulder: and his name shall be called Wonderful, Counsellor, The mighty God, The everlasting Father, The Prince of Peace" (Isaiah 9:6).

Many people have tried to capture in poetry and music the gratitude they feel to God. Sacred hymns fill our hearts with feelings of love and devotion and become prayers of gratitude that cannot be uttered in any other way. Spiritual music causes our hearts to swell wide "as all eternity" (Moses 7:41). Our souls are stirred when we sing such hymns as "I Believe in Christ," "How Great Thou Art," or "I Stand All Amazed":

I stand all amazed at the love Jesus offers me,
Confused at the grace that so fully he proffers me.

I tremble to know that for me he was crucified,
That for me, a sinner, he suffered, he bled and died.

I marvel that he would descend from his throne divine
To rescue a soul so rebellious and proud as mine,
That he should extend his great love unto such as I,
Sufficient to own, to redeem, and to justify.

I think of his hands pierced and bleeding to pay the debt!
Such mercy, such love, and devotion can I forget?
No, no, I will praise and adore at the mercy seat,
Until at the glorified throne I kneel at his feet.

Chorus:
Oh, it is wonderful that he should care for me
Enough to die for me!
Oh, it is wonderful, wonderful to me![8]

If you have ever been able to sing this or any other "song of redeeming love, I would ask, can ye feel so now?" (Alma 5:26).

NOTES

1. Matthews, *A Bible!* 290.
2. Talmage, "Parable of the Grateful Cat," 875–76.
3. McKay, Conference Report, April 1967, 86–87.
4. Smith, *Teachings of the Prophet Joseph Smith,* 137.
5. Packer, "Brilliant Morning of Forgiveness," 19–20.
6. Clark, Conference Report, October 1953, 84.
7. Maxwell, *Even As I Am,* 120.
8. *Hymns,* no. 193.

"EVEN AS I AM" 11

Come, follow me.
—Luke 18:22

The journey to become like Christ is the greatest reason for our sojourn in mortality. It is the primary purpose of mortal experience. Everything else is secondary. Hence the Savior's invitations (divine imperatives) to

"Look unto me" (Isaiah 45:22).
"Learn of me" (Matthew 11:29).
"Come, follow me" (Luke 18:22; Matthew 4:19).
"Do as I have done" (John 13:15).
"Come unto me" (Matthew 11:28).
"What manner of men ought ye to be? . . . even as I am" (3 Nephi 27:27).
"I am the way, the truth, the life" (John 14:6).
"I have set an example for you" (3 Nephi 18:16).

What manner of man is Christ? What is Heavenly Father like? President Heber C. Kimball answered: "I am perfectly satisfied that my Father and my God is a cheerful, pleasant, lively, and good-natured

Being. Why? Because I am cheerful, pleasant, lively, and good-natured when I have His Spirit. That is one reason why I know; and another is—the Lord said, through Joseph Smith, 'I delight in a glad heart and a cheerful countenance.' That arises from the perfection of His attributes; He is a jovial, lively person, and a beautiful man."[1] Christ's invitation to be like him is, therefore, an invitation to be happy.

COME UNTO CHRIST

The mission of the restored gospel is to "invite all to come unto Christ" (D&C 20:59) "and be perfected in him" (Moroni 10:32). Not only can we be with him in the next life but we can be precisely like him as well (Moroni 7:48).[2] He has assured us that in the eternities to come we will have power to do what he has done: "Verily, verily, I say unto you, He that believeth on me, the works that I do shall he do also; and greater works than these shall he do" (John 14:12).[3]

Obviously, we can be like him only if we learn more about him, receive his ordinances, and emulate his attributes. But becoming like him also means changing our hearts—experiencing what the scriptures call a "mighty change" of heart (Mosiah 5:2; Alma 5:13–14). It means making sure that what we understand in our minds about his nature and character, we plant in our hearts as well. The apostle Paul said that some are "ever learning, and never able to come to the knowledge of the truth" (2 Timothy 3:7). It is possible to acquire true religious knowledge without becoming more spiritual, but it is folly to try to know God apart from obeying his commandments, which will help us become more like him.

Knowledge is only one of the traits in Peter's list of eight qualities pertaining to life eternal and godliness that enable us to partake of the divine nature of Christ (2 Peter 1:5–7). In our technologically driven world, knowledge seems to matter most. The other traits Peter lists, however, include faith, virtue, temperance, patience, godliness, brotherly kindness, and charity. "For if these things be in you, and abound," wrote Peter, "they make you that ye shall neither be barren nor unfruitful in the knowledge of our Lord Jesus Christ. But he that lacketh these things is blind and cannot see afar off" (2 Peter 1:8–9). We need all of these attributes, not just knowledge. A revelation to the Prophet Joseph Smith reiterated the same cardinal virtues and celestial traits as Peter did and added three more: humility, diligence, and an eye single to the glory of God (D&C 4:4–6).[4] Lives filled with faith, virtue, temperance, patience, godliness, kindness, pure love, humility, and diligence with an eye single to the glory of God are Christlike lives.

BECOMING PERFECT

Jesus said, "If ye love me, keep my commandments" (John 14:15). The most overwhelming of his commandments is "be perfect even as I, or your Father who is in heaven is perfect" (3 Nephi 12:48). Ultimate perfection—Christlike perfection—is an eternal goal, not a mortal possibility. Christlike perfection necessarily involves a process extending throughout life and beyond the grave. The Prophet Joseph Smith indicated that it will be long after the resurrection before we reach that glorified state.[5]

Christlike living, on the other hand, is possible. When he commanded us to become perfect, as he is, he was referring to the way as well as to the end result. He challenges us to speed up the process, to not delay the effort. He promises us that he will help us (Ether 12:27). "Yea, come unto Christ, and be perfected in him, and deny yourselves of all ungodliness; and if ye shall deny yourselves of all ungodliness, and love God with all your might, mind and strength, then is his grace sufficient for you, that by his grace ye may be perfect in Christ; and if by the grace of God ye are perfect in Christ, ye can in nowise deny the power of God.

"And again, if ye by the grace of God are perfect in Christ, and deny not his power, then are ye sanctified in Christ by the grace of God, through the shedding of the blood of Christ, which is in the covenant of the Father unto the remission of your sins, that ye become holy, without spot" (Moroni 10:32–33).

President Spencer W. Kimball described what it means to be "holy, without spot": "To be like Christ! What an ambitious goal! What a lofty ideal! The Savior had a pleasing personality, he was kind, he was pleasant, he was understanding, he never went off on tangents, he was perfectly balanced. No eccentricities could be found in his life. Here was no ostentation and show, but he was real and humble and genuine. He made no play for popularity. He made no compromises to gain favor. He did the right thing always, regardless of how it might appeal to men. He drew all good people to him as a magnet.

"'What manner of men ought ye to be?' The answer, 'Even as I am,' means that one must be forgiving, there must be no grudges, no hatreds, no bitterness. . . .

"To be like him, then, one must resist evil. One must fortify one's self by keeping away from temptation, out of the devil's area. One must control desire, harness passion, bridle every urge, and keep away from the approach of error. Total cleanliness in thought and action is required if one is to be Christlike."[6]

In a day-to-day existence, that still may seem a lofty goal. Yet, the Savior and his prophets have assured us that it is an attainable one. So where do we begin? We start by following the example of the Savior: "Behold I am the light; I have set an example for you" (3 Nephi 8:16). Some things Jesus did that we can do are as follows:[7]

He loved and obeyed his Father (Matthew 26:39; John 5:19, 30).

He understood his calling and his authority (John 10:7–15; 13:3).

He prayed and studied the scriptures (Matthew 14:23; Luke 4:4; 24:27).

He taught and performed the ordinances of salvation (John 3:22).

He taught people about the Holy Spirit and urged them to heed the Spirit's promptings (John 14:16–26).

He admonished his followers to consecrate their time and talents to God's work, especially to serving others (Matthew 19:16–26).

He taught people to repent and forgive (Matthew 5–8; 18:21–22; Luke 15:11–32).

He taught and led people according to their capacity and potential, asking enough of them to stretch their souls but not so much that they were overwhelmed with more than they could handle (Matthew 13:10–13).

He taught people to observe the fast (Matthew 6:16–18; Mark 9:29).

He taught people to donate tithes and offerings (3 Nephi 24:1–11).

He expressed love, compassion, understanding, and appreciation for the people he led (Matthew 9:36; 20:34; 26:6–13).

He dedicated his life to helping people return to the Father's presence (Matthew 4:17).

He ministered personally to his people, knowing them individually and walking and working among them (Matthew 4:23–24; 3 Nephi 18:31).

He was not condescending to others, although he was the only perfect mortal (Luke 19:2–9; John 4:6–42).

He recognized the potential of others and called them to help in the work of his kingdom (Matthew 10).

He respected individual agency by teaching correct principles, allowing personal governance, and providing an opportunity to account for individual actions (Matthew 10).

He condemned sin without condemning the sinner (John 8:3–11).

He ministered to both the repentant and the unrepentant.

He lifted the downtrodden and gave hope to the discouraged (John 16:33; 3 Nephi 1:10–13).

He listened.

He considered short-range and long-range perspectives when dealing with people and their problems.

He blessed the sick.

He cared for the poor and needy.

To live in the world without God in our lives, said Alma, is "contrary to the nature of happiness" (Alma 41:11). "As for such souls, their mortal lives are 'no more than a night in a second-class hotel.' (Saint Teresa of Avila.)."8 But with Christ as our Guide—by following his example—this second estate can be a real first-class experience.

President Gordon B. Hinckley testified: "You will find your greatest example in the Son of God. I hope that each of you will make Him your friend. I hope you will strive to walk in His paths, extending mercy, blessing those who struggle, living with less selfishness, reaching out to others.

" . . . During His brief ministry, He brought more of truth, more of hope, more of mercy, more of love than anyone else who has walked the earth. He died on Calvary's cross for each of us. He arose the third day. . . .

" . . . He was the great paragon of righteousness, the only perfect man ever to walk the earth. His was the wondrous example toward whom each of us might point our lives in our eternal quest for excellence.

" . . . 'Look to God and live' (Alma 37:47). Kneel before Him in supplication. He will help you. He will bless you. He will comfort and sustain you."⁹

"THAT WILL DEPEND ENTIRELY UPON YOURSELF"

In 1876, Elder Orson F. Whitney was called on a mission to Pennsylvania. About that time he had a remarkable dream, which taught him that becoming like Christ and spending the next life with Christ in the celestial kingdom was a choice we have the ability to make. He related the dream in these words:

"I thought I was in the garden of Gethsemane, a witness of the Savior's agony. I seemed to be standing behind a tree in the foreground of the picture, from which point I could see without being seen. The Savior, with the Apostles Peter, James and John, entered the garden through a little wicket gate at my right, where he stationed them in a group, telling them to pray. He then passed over to my left, but still in front of me, where he knelt and prayed also. His face, which was towards me, streamed with tears, as he besought the Father to let the cup pass, and added, 'not my will but thine be done.' Having finished his prayer, he arose and crossed to where the Apostles were kneeling fast asleep. He shook them gently, they awoke and he reproved them for their apathy. Again he bade them pray, and again crossed to his place and prayed, returning as before to find them sleeping. This happened three times, until I was perfectly familiar with his face, form and movements. He was much taller than ordinary men, and though meek, far more dignified than any being I had ever beheld; and he wore a look of ineffable tenderness and compassion, even while reproving His disciples. My heart went out to him as never before to anybody or to anything; I loved him with all my soul. I wept at seeing him weep, and felt for him the deepest sympathy. Then of a sudden the circumstances changed, though the scene remained the same. Instead of before the crucifixion, it was after. The Savior and the three Apostles, whom he had beckoned to him, now stood in a group at the left, and were about to take their departure, ascending into heaven. I could endure it no longer, but rushed out from behind the tree, fell at his feet, clasped him around the knees and begged him to take me also. With a look of infinite tenderness, as of a father or an elder brother, he stooped, lifted me up and embraced me, saying as he did so in the kindest and gentlest manner possible, while slowly shaking his head and sweetly smiling, 'No, my son, these can go with me; for they have finished their work; but you must stay and finish yours!' Still I clung to him, and the contact was so real that I felt the warmth of his bosom as I rested upon it. Gazing up into his face, I once more besought him, 'Well, promise me that I will come to you at the last.' Again he smiled sweetly, and there was a look as if he would have gladly granted my request had it been wise to do so. He then said, 'That will depend entirely upon yourself.' I awoke with a sob, and it was morning."[10]

Christ's final hours on earth opened the door for us all to experience eternal possibilities. With him, all things are possible to those who believe. And when our faith is centered in him, all blessings are possible: "I give unto you these sayings that you may understand and know how to worship, and know what you worship, that you may come unto the Father in my name, and in due time receive of his fulness. For if you keep my commandments you shall receive of his fulness, and be glorified in me as I am in the Father" (D&C 93:19–20).

NOTES

1. Kimball, *Journal of Discourses*, 4:222.
2. Smith, *Lectures on Faith*, 7:9.

3. *Lectures on Faith* indicates that John 14:12 refers to the works we will do in the next life rather than the works we do in this life.

4. Smith, *History of the Church,* 4:163.

5. Ehat and Cook, *Words of Joseph Smith,* 345, 348.

6. Kimball, *Teachings of Spencer W. Kimball,* 13.

7. "Savior's Righteous Leadership Sets Example for Today."

8. Maxwell, *Notwithstanding My Weakness,* 27–28.

9. Hinckley, "Quest for Excellence," 5.

10. Jenson, *LDS Biographical Encyclopedia,* 1:658.

SOURCES CONSULTED
SOURCES CONSULTED

Abingdon Bible Commentary. Edited by Frederick Carl Eiselen, Edwin Lewis, and David G. Downey. New York and Nashville: Abingdon Press, 1929.

Ballard, Melvin J. *Crusader for Righteousness.* Salt Lake City: Bookcraft, 1966.

Benson, Ezra Taft. "Beware of Pride." *Ensign,* May 1989.

———. Conference Report, April 1977.

———. Conference Report, April 1982.

Clark, J. Reuben, Jr. Conference Report, October 1953.

Clawson, Rudger. Conference Report, October 1908.

Deseret News Semi-Weekly. Salt Lake City, 28 July 1874. In *Brigham Young.* Teachings of Presidents of the Church Series. Salt Lake City: The Church of Jesus Christ of Latter-day Saints, 1997.

Devitry-Smith, John. "The Saint and the Grave Robber." *Brigham Young University Studies* 33, 1 (1993).

Ehat, Andrew F., and Lyndon W. Cook, eds. *Words of Joseph Smith.* Provo, Utah: Brigham Young University, 1980.

Gospel Principles. Salt Lake City: The Church of Jesus Christ of Latter-day Saints, 1992.

Hafen, Bruce C., and Marie K. Hafen. "'Eve Heard All These Things and Was Glad': Grace and Learning by Experience." In Dawn Hall

Anderson and Susette Fletcher Green, eds. *Women in the Covenant of Grace: Talks Selected from the 1993 Women's Conference.* Salt Lake City: Deseret Book, 1994.

Hamilton, Edith. *Spokesman for God.* New York: W. W. Norton, 1936.

Hinckley, Gordon B. "The Quest for Excellence." *Ensign,* September 1999.

————. "Reach Out in Love and Kindness." *Ensign,* November 1982.

————. "Rejoice in This Great Era of Temple Building." *Ensign,* November 1985.

Holland, Jeffrey R. "I Stand All Amazed." *Ensign,* August 1986.

Hunter, Howard W. Conference Report, October 1960.

————. Conference Report, April 1986.

————. "He Invites Us to Follow Him." *Ensign,* September 1994.

Hymns of The Church of Jesus Christ of Latter-day Saints. Salt Lake City: The Church of Jesus Christ of Latter-day Saints, 1985.

Jenson, Andrew. *LDS Biographical Encyclopedia.* 4 vols. Salt Lake City: Andrew Jenson Memorial Association, 1936.

Journal of Discourses. 26 vols. London: Latter-day Saints' Book Depot, 1854–86.

Kimball, Spencer W. *The Miracle of Forgiveness.* Salt Lake City: Bookcraft, 1969.

————. *The Teachings of Spencer W. Kimball.* Edited by Edward L. Kimball. Salt Lake City: Bookcraft, 1982.

Lee, Harold B. *Divine Revelation.* Brigham Young University Speeches of the Year, Provo, Utah, 15 October 1952.

————. "'Stand Ye in Holy Places.'" *Ensign,* July 1973.

Lewis, C. S. *Mere Christianity.* New York: Macmillan, 1952.

Ludlow, Daniel H. "The Greatest Week in History." *Ensign,* April 1972.

Matthews, Robert J. *A Bible! A Bible!* Salt Lake City: Bookcraft, 1990.

Maxwell, Neal A. *Even As I Am.* Salt Lake City: Deseret Book, 1982.

————. *Lord, Increase Our Faith.* Salt Lake City: Bookcraft, 1994.

————. *Men and Women of Christ.* Salt Lake City: Bookcraft, 1991.

————. *Not My Will, But Thine.* Salt Lake City: Bookcraft, 1988.

————. *Notwithstanding My Weakness.* Salt Lake City: Deseret Book, 1981.

———. *One More Strain of Praise.* Salt Lake City: Bookcraft, 1999.

———. *O How Great the Plan of Our God!* Address to CES religious educators, 3 February 1995. Salt Lake City: The Church of Jesus Christ of Latter-day Saints, 1995.

———. "'A Brother Offended.'" *Ensign,* May 1982.

———. Conference Report, April 1976.

———. Conference Report, April 1987.

———. "'Willing to Submit.'" *Ensign,* May 1985.

McConkie, Bruce R. *Mormon Doctrine.* Salt Lake City: Bookcraft, 1966.

———. *The Mortal Messiah.* 4 vols. Salt Lake City: Deseret Book, 1979–81.

———. *A New Witness for the Articles of Faith.* Salt Lake City: Deseret Book, 1985.

———. *The Promised Messiah.* Salt Lake City: Deseret Book, 1978.

———. "The Bible, a Sealed Book." In *A Symposium on the New Testament.* Prepared by the Church Educational System. Salt Lake City: The Church of Jesus Christ of Latter-day Saints, 1984.

McKay, David O. Conference Report, October 1950.

———. Conference Report, April 1951.

———. Conference Report, April 1967.

Murphy-O'Connor, Jerome. *The Holy Land: An Archaeological Guide from Earliest Times to 1700.* 3d ed. New York: Oxford University Press, 1992.

Millet, Robert L. *Selected Writings of Robert L. Millet.* Salt Lake City: Deseret Book, 2000.

Oaks, Dallin H. "'Judge Not' and Judging." *Ensign,* August 1999.

Old Testament: Genesis–2 Samuel [Religion 301 student manual]. Prepared by the Church Educational System. Salt Lake City: The Church of Jesus Christ of Latter-day Saints, 1981.

Packer, Boyd K. "The Brilliant Morning of Forgiveness." *Ensign,* November 1995.

Reynolds, George, and Janne M. Sjodahl. *Commentary on the Book of Mormon.* 7 vols. Salt Lake City: Deseret Book, 1955–61.

"Savior's Righteous Leadership Sets Example for Today." *Church News,* 11 May 1991.

Sherry, Thomas E. "Christ, Savior, Son of God—As Revealed in the Joseph Smith Translation." Presentation given at the Christ, Savior, Son of God Symposium. Brigham Young University, Provo, Utah, 8 January 2000.

Skinner, Andrew C. "Restored Light on the Savior's Last Week in Mortality." *Ensign,* June 1999.

Smith, Joseph. *History of The Church of Jesus Christ of Latter-day Saints.* Edited by B. H. Roberts. 2d ed. rev. 7 vols. Salt Lake City: The Church of Jesus Christ of Latter-day Saints, 1932–51.

———. *Lectures on Faith.* Compiled by N. B. Lundwall. Salt Lake City: N. B. Lundwall, n. d.

———. *Teachings of the Prophet Joseph Smith.* Selected by Joseph Fielding Smith. Salt Lake City: Deseret Book, 1976.

Smith, Joseph F. *Gospel Doctrine.* 5th ed. Salt Lake City: Deseret Book, 1939.

Smith, Joseph Fielding. *Doctrines of Salvation.* 3 vols. Compiled by Bruce R. McConkie. Salt Lake City: Bookcraft, 1954–56.

———. *The Progress of Man.* Salt Lake City: Deseret Book, 1964.

———. Conference Report, October 1918.

Snow, Lorenzo. Conference Report, October 1900.

Talmage, James E. *Jesus the Christ.* Salt Lake City: Deseret Book, 1976.

———. "The Parable of the Grateful Cat." *Improvement Era,* August 1916.

Watson, Elden J., comp. *Manuscript History of Brigham Young, 1846–1847.* Salt Lake City: Smith Secretarial Service, 1971.

Welch, John W. "The Good Samaritan: A Type and Shadow of the Plan of Salvation." *Brigham Young University Studies* 38, 2 (1999).

Widtsoe, John A. "The Worth of Souls." *Utah Genealogical and Historical Magazine* 25 (October 1934).

Weatherhead, Leslie D. "When I Am Tempted." In *Christ's Ideals for Living.* Salt Lake City: Deseret Sunday School Union Board, 1955.

INDEX

Darkness, 77–78; powers of, 54, 58
Day of Judgment, 106
Days, holy, 24
Dead, gospel preached to, 89
Death, 86; power over, 1; of Savior, 2; and Christ, 4; physical, 10, 98; spiritual, 10, 67, 82; angel of, 40; powers of, 54
Debt, payment of, 44
Denial, Peter's, 62
Diligence, 113
Disappointment, 33
Discipleship, 6
Dome of the Rock, 22

Earth, 2, 87
Emblems of the sacrament, 36
Empathy, 48, 50–51
Endurance, 66
Enemies, love of, 55
Eternal life, 1, 4; hope for, 18
Eternity, 87
Exaltation, 14; of Christ, 3

Faith, 112–13, 117
Fall, the, 15
Father, the, 20
Feast of Tabernacles, 22
Feet, washing of, 29
Forgiveness, 36; gift of, 9
Forsakenness, 78

Game of kings, 67
Gehenna, 21
Gethsemane, 21; Garden of, 42, 47–48; and Satan, 46; visions of, 52–53
Gift(s): of forgiveness, 9; of mercy, 13; of God, 101
Gilead, balm of, 43
God, the Father, 20
Godliness, 112–13
Golden Gate, 22
Golgotha, 83
Gospel, 56; preached to dead, 86, 89; acceptance of, 88; preaching of, 91; mission of restored, 112

Gospels, the, as testimonies, 6–7
Grace, throne of, 50
Grand Council, 12
Granger, Oliver, 104
Gratitude, 104, 107; hymns of, 109

Hallel, 37–40
Hamilton, Edith, 56
Handicaps, mental, 49
Happiness, plan of, 7, 115
Heart, broken, 82
Heavenly Father: following, 33; kingdom of, 44; presence of, 81; reuniting with the Son, 96; love and gifts of, 101; and service, 103; return to presence of, 108; nature of, 111. *See also* God
Hematodrosis, 48
Herod, palace of, 64; Christ before, 65–66
High Priestly Prayer, 33
Hinckley, Gordon B., 15; on vicarious work, 90; on example of Son of God, 115–16
History, family, 91–92
Holland, Jeffrey R.: on heavenly reunion, 96
Holy days, 24
Holy Ghost, 32; reception of, 3; and revelation, 28; withdrawal of, 80; witness of, 101
Holy of Holies, 33–34, 81
Hope, 1; for eternal life, 18
Hosanna Shout, 22
Humility, 29, 105, 113
Hunter, Howard W.: on knowing Christ, 5–6; on the resurrection, 94
Hurst, Charles, 90
Hurst, Frederick William, 90
Hymns, 109

Immortality, 98–99
Ingratitude, 102
Injustice, 55, 69
Isaac, sacrifice of, 72
Israelites, latter-day, 14

ideal, 3; on love of God, 30
Mercy, 10, 48, 50, 107; gift of, 13
Messiah, 22–24
Millet, Robert L., 54–55
Miracles, 6; seeking of, 65; of
    resurrection, 99
Mockery, 67, 75
Mormon, half-hearted, 18
Mortality, purpose of, 111
Moses, 82; and serpent of brass, 76
Mount Moriah, 72
Mount of Olives, 42
Music, sacred, 37

Nephites, 107
Nicodemus, 83

Oaks, Dallin H., 56
Oil, olive, 42–43
Only Begotten Son of God, 13
Ordinances, 29, 88; temple, 15;
    vicarious priesthood, 87, 89; and
    becoming Christlike, 112

Packer, Boyd K., 106
Pain, 50
Palace of Annas, 58–60
Palm Sunday, 22
Parable, 25; of good Samaritan,
    16–17; of the grateful cat, 102–3
Paradise, 76, 87
Passover, 27, 67; final, 35–36, 40;
    symbols of, 55
Patience, 112–13
Peace, 9; Prince of, 22; inner, 101
Perdition, sons of, 14
Perfection: way to, 2; of Saints, 16;
    Christlike, 113
Persecution, 73
Peter, 58; defense of Christ, 57;
    denial of Christ, 62
Plan of salvation, 11–12, 14, 16, 86;
    and provisions for all, 89
Pontius Pilate, 63–64; Christ's
    second appearance before, 66;
    washing of hands of, 69
Possibilities, eternal, 117

Potter's field, 63
Power: of Christ, 6; over all things,
    51–52; of death and darkness, 54
Prayer: High Priestly, 33;
    intercessory, 34; and trials, 47;
    answers to, 107
Pride, 106
Priests, chief, hypocrisy of the,
    59–61
Prince of Peace, 22
Principles, eternal, 2
Prison, spirit, 85, 87–88
Prophets, 16, 18
Punishment, 44, 63

Rebirth, 44, 82
Redeemer, 1
Redemption, 12–13
Remission of sin, 82
Repentance, 10, 82, 88
Responsibility, 15
Resurrection, 15, 87; of Christ,
    9–10, 94, 96–99; as reunion, 96;
    eyewitness accounts of, 97;
    physical blessings of, 99; celestial,
    99
Revelation, 28
Reverence, 105–6
Righteousness, peaceable fruit of, 51

Sabbath, the, 81
Sacrament, 35–36
Sacrifice, 1, 104; symbolic, 28; of
    Isaac, 72
Saints: perfection of, 16; testimonies
    of latter-day, 98
Salvation: plan of, 11–12, 14, 16,
    86; eternal, 15; and provisions
    for all, 89
Samaritan, parable of good, 16–17
Sanctification, 113
Sanhedrin, 58–59
Satan, 76; rebellion of, 12; as
    unclean spirit, 15; and Judas
    Iscariot, 31; in Garden of
    Gethsemane, 46–47; and